SUNNIE

(but partly cloudy)

40 years of life changing

choices and answered

prayers

Eliza Beth Lee

1

Most proper names in my story have been changed or altered, so as not to offend anyone who is part of my story.

This is a creative autobiography of my life...

from my perspective...

Chapters of My Life...

...to be continued

Acknowledgments

Most importantly, I want to thank God for saving my life and continually answering my prayers, even when I may not be doing His will; for without His intervention in my life, I would not be here to share my story.

I would also like to thank all my family and friends who encouraged me to write down my memories, thoughts, and feelings—even if it was originally just for my own therapy.

I want to thank each one of my Beta readers—both here and overseas—for each editing suggestion you contributed. I may not have made as many changes as some of you suggested, but *getting in touch with my feelings* helped me more than you will ever know.

I especially want to thank Kate Kindred, who saw a story amidst my written memories and offered to help make this book a reality.

Lastly, I want to thank the man who helps me survive in my every day life, my husband—without his constant support over the past several years, this never would have been possible. Thank you for putting up with my changing moods and my panic attacks and for always staying calm when I stress out!

I love you all!

Chapter 1

My coma
1978

I hear voices.

Mom and Dad. Leigh and Edward. How can that be?
They all live in different places. How can they all be in the
same room at the same time? They are talking to me, and
they sound so concerned. They ask me if I can hear them.
My sister asks me to squeeze her hand. My brother is
asking me if I'm okay. My dad lays his hand on my
shoulder, "Wake up, Eliza," he says. My mom is crying; I
can hear her trying to speak to me, but she can barely talk.

I can hear them, but why can't I respond to them? Why
can't I see them?

And then I realize I can see them; not around me, but below
me. I'm looking down on them as they stand over me. I'm
lying in a bed, and they are holding my hands, asking me if
I can hear them. I try to squeeze their hands, but I can't!

They ask me to do something, anything, to show that I can
hear them; but I can't move, can't speak, can't even blink
my eyes.

How can it be that I am looking down on my family? Where are we, and what is going on? It's too much for me to comprehend.

I'm frustrated. I'm so tired.

And then they are gone.

Again, I hear voices. This time it's different voices, but one I recognize. It is Dan's voice, my cousin's boyfriend. I only met him recently. Why is he here? He is introducing me to someone named Pete. I can't see them, but I can hear them. They are talking to me, and they say they don't know if I can hear them, but they keep talking as though they think I can. Dan says he has brought me some Chapstick because I keep licking my dry lips. I feel the balm pressing against my lips, but I still can't see anything.

Why is he doing this? Why are people talking to me and treating me like I'm a child? Why are they so concerned?

Why do they ask me to respond, to open my eyes and look at them? Why can I hear them, but not see them? Why can't I speak?

"We aren't supposed to be in your room, but we snuck in to see you again while we are visiting Anne," Dan says. I don't understand what they are talking about. Why aren't they allowed here? Where am I? And why is Anne here, too?

Now they say goodbye and tell me they have to leave before they get caught.

I'm confused. I'm so tired. I drift back into my comfortable sleep.

Distant voices wake me again. This time I can see, though things look foggy.

There is a large poster on the wall, a small stuffed animal in my arms. But the walls around me are unfamiliar, and there is a white curtain at the end of my bed.

Where am I? Where is my family?

"Help me!" I call out. But my voice seems to only be inside of my head; no sound escapes from my lips, no one answers me.

Why can't I talk? Why can't I move?

The voices that woke me are closer now, beyond the curtain; but they are unfamiliar. I hear them discussing a young girl who needs surgery. "We cannot perform surgery until she is fully awake and out of her coma," one female voice says. Another says they have no way of knowing when that will be. "So far, she has shown no signs of life, but our tests show brain activity," a male voice says.

Are they talking about me?

"Hello!" I call out, again. But my voice is still silent, and no one answers me.

I'm just so tired. I can feel myself beginning to drift back to sleep. The voices beyond the curtain are gone now.

The next time I awaken, I am being rolled out of the room with the curtain and out into a hallway. I see my mom standing there, and she smiles at me. She is talking to me, but the person rolling my bed down the hallway keeps pushing me past her.

"After your surgery, you'll get your own room!" It's all I hear. I don't know what she is talking about...I try to reply, but I have no energy, I have no voice. Once again, I feel myself drifting away...

I am awake again. I am in another small room with a white curtain around the bed. Where is the poster? Where is the stuffed animal I held in my arms? Where am I?

I don't want to sleep anymore! I don't want to dream anymore! Why won't anyone here talk to me and tell me what is happening? Why can't I talk or move? Did I really just see my mom, or is all of this just part of my dream that I can't escape?

I am trying to stay awake, trying to speak; but the words must be only in my head because no one seems to hear me.

A nurse comes into my little room, and she is checking the tube going into my arm. More nurses enter the room, but not one of them talks to me.

Now they are rolling my bed out into a hallway again, into an elevator, and out into another hallway. As they wheel me into another room, we pass a restroom; and I see a couch up against the wall of the room with a pillow and blanket lying upon it—someone has been sleeping there. By the window is an empty hospital bed. I see the same poster on the wall I saw before, but this can't be the same room as the one with the curtain because this room has a couch, and this room is much bigger than the one I remember. I'm so confused!

The nurses roll me parallel to the hospital bed, and I feel several hands lift me and scoop me onto it. One of the nurses hooks the tube connected to my arm to a bag on a pole. I hear her ask someone if we need anything else.

I turn my head and see my mom sitting on the couch. She must be the one who has been sleeping there, but for how long? I must not be fully awake yet because I didn't see her there when we came into the room.

Why isn't anyone talking to me?

My mom thanks the nurses for their help. Then she stands and approaches my bed.

"Eliza, can you hear me? Are you in pain? You just had surgery on your jaw. It was broken. Do you remember what happened?"

This is all too much for me to comprehend, and I can't answer her. Her words are just all running together in my head.

I try to shake my head, *No*. I try to tell her "No," but I cannot talk; all that comes out is a raspy whisper. She returns to the couch. I close my eyes and try to listen to her talk, but I fall asleep again.

Once again, I awaken to an unfamiliar voice; and a nurse is standing over me, asking me if I'd like to watch the television. I whisper, "Yes," my voice still rough, but at least I was heard; and it's not just inside of my head. She turns the television on, the volume turned low. I look toward the couch and see my mother is there, asleep. I don't even know what time of the day or night it is.

The nurse takes the IV needle out of my arm, applies a band-aide, and tells me I will be able to have some liquids today. "How about a chocolate milkshake," she asks? I nod enthusiastically—or at least I think I do.

She smiles, sets the remote control on the table next to the bed and leaves the room.

I look up at the television and a commercial is playing.

I struggle to reach over and pick up the remote and begin to press buttons, hoping to find something else to watch.

Maybe if I can find a familiar television show I know, it will help me figure out if it is daytime or nighttime.

I wish the blinds were open so I could see where I am—so I could see if its day or night—it's so claustrophobic in here.

I push the channel *up* button and recognize a program, but the channels keep changing.

I passed the show I wanted to watch, and I can't remember the channel number, so I press the channel *down* button. I end up passing the show again. I know that I can use a television remote, but I can't stop pushing the buttons in time to stop on a channel.

This is so frustrating! What is wrong with me?

"Mom?" My voice still sounds harsh as I call out to her.

She wakes up and sits up quickly. "What do you need, Sunnie?"

It comforts me to hear my nickname. I try to hand her the remote, she reaches over and takes it out of my hand. She presses one of the buttons and slowly sifts through the channels. She stops on an episode of Black Sheep Squadron that seems to just be starting.

My mom rarely watches television, but this is a show we both like. "Peter Frampton," I whisper. I recognize him on the television and realize that he is also the person on the poster in my room. My mom knows I am a Peter Frampton fan, but I'm not sure she realizes he is in this episode of the show.

She is not happy about me being a fan of some long-haired rock star; but the fact that she has allowed someone to hang what seems like a life size Peter Frampton poster on the wall of my hospital room, is clearly an indication that whatever has happened to me was serious.

Not realizing I'm referring to the television show, she turns and nods at the poster. "Your sister brought that for you when you were in Intensive Care." She turns back to me and smiles. "The doctors and the nurses have told us that having familiar items around you, or watching familiar television shows, may help you to remember."

Remember?

What is she referring to that I don't remember?

What is it that has happened to me?

My mom has returned to her place on the couch; perhaps she does not want to discuss whatever it is or is hoping I'll remember on my own.

I turn my attention back to the television, knowing it will distract me from these frustrating thoughts.

And then my first milkshake is delivered.

Because of my jaw surgery, I am told I can't use a straw yet but will instead have to use a spoon to eat. I don't know how long I've been in the hospital, but it's clear this is the first real food I've had since I arrived. My mom comes over to my bed again and is holding the cup and the spoon as though she is going to feed me—it makes me feel like a child. I take the spoon from her and try to feed myself. I hold the spoon and scoop a little bit of frozen milkshake out of the cup and try to bring it to my mouth, but the milkshake spills on my clean white sheet. I try again and miss my mouth entirely. Why is this so difficult? What has happened that has caused me to not even be able to feed myself? I don't want to have to ask for help. I try again and manage to get a small spoonful of milkshake between my lips. My jaw is wired together; and I can barely open my mouth, but it stills tastes so good!

It takes me a long time; but while we watch Black Sheep Squadron, I finish most of it.

When I am done eating, my mom takes the almost empty cup, and I return my attention to the television; but the difficulty of feeding myself and my inability to remember how I ended up here is leaving me frustrated and tired.

I lay back and close my eyes, listening to the voices on the television. I hear Peter Frampton's voice.

Now I'm dreaming…

I'm back in high school, attending a Peter Frampton concert. Leigh and Anne are with me. We have lost our blanket and Leigh is asking some guys we just met if we can share their blanket with them—I was embarrassed—of course, the guys say, "Yes." What young men wouldn't want a blonde model sharing their blanket with them…

Anne and I are just along for the ride.

When I awake again, my mom is sleeping. I have to pee, but I hate the bedpan, and I don't want to have to call a nurse for help. I'm not hooked up to the IV anymore, so there's no reason I shouldn't be able to get to the toilet on my own.

I know I can do this.

I push myself up, so I'm seated on the bed. I'm a little dizzy, but I'm sure I'll be okay once I stand. I slowly dangle my legs over the side of the bed and sit there for a moment. I start sliding down toward the floor. I stand up and hold on to the bed rail. It's not until my feet are planted on the floor that I realize I probably haven't stood on them since I arrived—although I really have no idea how long ago that was.

The restroom is only a few feet away, how difficult can it be to get over there? I take one step, then two and collapse on the floor.

My mom wakes up and sees me, rushing to my side and calling for a nurse, who seems to arrive immediately. I'm on the floor, crying, apologizing for waking up my mom, apologizing for not making it to the toilet. They get me up and to the restroom, change me into a clean gown, and then walk me back to the bed.

I realize it's going to be a while before I can do much of anything without help.

As the days go on, I have little concept of time. I'm not sure how long I've been here, I can't keep track of the number of days since my surgery and my mom keeps asking me if I remember what happened. I just stare at her, confused, not knowing how to answer her questions, because I don't remember anything about what landed me here.

I'm so confused by the fact that I can barely eat and barely talk or walk, and why won't anyone just tell me what happened?

Chapter 2

Mom's explanation

Eventually, my mother explains to me that I am in a hospital in Jackson, Mississippi; and that my cousin, Anne, and I had been in a car accident. It is such a relief to have a piece of the puzzle! Now I understand that the visit from Anne's boyfriend, Dan, was not a dream.

"Anne has been released from the hospital, with some cuts and bruises; she also had a dislocated hip," my mom tells me. She then tells me that I was in a coma, and once out of it, I had to have my broken jaw repaired; now I need to remain in the hospital to recover from my surgery.

Although I now understand why I am here, I still do not understand exactly what happened. It's all just too much to try to comprehend.

"How long was I in a coma, mom?"

She hesitates and then replies, "I think about nine days."

How long have I been here, I wonder? Why are we in Mississippi?

My mother seems to sense my confusion and little by little provides me with additional information; but her story is intermingled with, "Do you remember any of this?" To which I mostly answer, "No".

I sense that before anyone is willing to explain too much, they are hoping to compare Anne's story to mine— something that had happened quite often during our high school years.

I can't recall the last time I was in a vehicle with Anne— not since we were in high school together, maybe; how was it we ended up in a car accident in Mississippi? What exactly happened that put us both in a hospital, so messed up? Was anyone else hurt in the accident? What happened to Anne's car?

These are all questions I want to ask my mom, but I hesitate because it's all just too much for me to comprehend at this time. All these questions are in my head, but I have a hard time saying much of anything.

My mom tells me that Anne and I were in an accident on the Natchez Trace Parkway, just outside of Jackson. (I later learn that the road is referred to as "The Trace," and is a two-lane, tree-lined scenic Parkway that begins in Natchez, Mississippi and ends in Nashville, Tennessee.)

She also reminds me that we drove on The Trace on our way to Northern Mississippi, but it was dark then; so I probably don't remember it.

She asks if I remember driving back down The Trace with Anne, towards Jackson. I shake my head, 'No'.

I learned that my mother and I drove to Northern Mississippi to visit some of our family for the Easter holiday and my spring break. It was not yet Anne's spring break, and so the two of us were going to travel back to Southern Mississippi for a few days, where Anne attended Whitworth College. The accident occurred on our way there. To my surprise, my mother then reveals that she was told I was the one driving the car when the accident happened! And we were in my mom's car, not Anne's car!

Confusion is setting in again. Why was I driving? Anne always drove when we were together. I didn't even get my license until the last semester of my senior year.

Is it still my senior year?

How long have I been in Mississippi?

How long have I been in the hospital?

My mom answers some of my questions, some she does not. I seem to be asking the same questions over and over again because I can't remember her answers.

After she tells me a few things, I do remember riding with my mom to visit our relatives and my friend, June, during our trip to Mississippi. June was attending an Academy in Northern Mississippi, where my mom's family lived. We arrived at night, and I got to go see June in her dorm when we got there. June, who was a member of the Academy choir, invited me to go to a high school choir competition at Mississippi State University the next day. I don't remember if they won the competition, but I remember they sounded great!

I also remember going back to her dorm and making marshmallow Rice Krispy treats that night.

How long ago was that, I wonder?

I am so frustrated, and I am so confused.

I can't remember anything since that day we arrived in Mississippi, and I can't seem to get an answer as to when that was. I ask my mom again how long we have been in Mississippi and wait for her to answer.

She hesitates and changes the subject.

My thoughts are interrupted by news that I have visitors.

I thought everyone except my mom had returned home— who else would come to see me?

I'm worried as to whom it might be; I don't really want anyone else to see me, looking like this. I realize I haven't been able to bathe or wash my hair during my hospital stay, and the broken jaw and subsequent surgery have caused my face to be horribly bruised and swollen.

When two boys walk into my hospital room, it takes me a moment to remember them. I first recognize Paul, June's boyfriend; but then I recognize Joe too, another friend of ours from Florida.

At first, I'm stunned to see them, but then my brain begins calculations; if they are here, maybe it's still spring break, which means its possible I haven't been in the hospital that long. But my mom told me I was in a coma for nine days…now, I am really confused.

They tell me they were visiting June at the Academy in Northern Mississippi and heard about my accident. Joe steps closer to the bed to talk to me, and I worry what my mom is going to think about a boy visiting me who she doesn't even know.

I never really introduced my mom to any of the boys I hung out with. Maybe more so because I can't really say I *dated* a lot of boys in the traditional sense, most of my social activity when it came to boys was simply *hanging out* together at parties or other social gatherings.

While Paul was June's boyfriend and went to our church, Joe was someone I had been *hanging out with* recently—at least from what I could remember. *He isn't really my type, but he is very nice—and I think he has a crush on me.* I was still very self-conscious about the way I looked, but seeing familiar faces of friends from Florida was a pleasant surprise, so I didn't really care much.

Joe was kind and sympathetic toward my injuries. It was obvious he wasn't exactly sure what all had happened to me, but he didn't ask too many questions.

The two of them were on their way back to Florida; but since June told them I had been in an accident and recovering in a hospital in Jackson, they decided to stop on their way through town.

I discovered it was their spring break, but then they explained that because we were in different school districts, their break had come after mine. This provided a few more clues to the timeline; my hospital stay had indeed been longer than the week of my spring break.

After a bit of small talk, Joe told me he hoped he'd see me again soon, and the two of them left.

Later, when my mother asked me about Joe, I simply told her he was a friend of Paul's that I just had met before at a party.

Being from our church, she already knew Paul, so my explanation regarding Joe seemed to suffice. "Well, it was very nice of them to take the time to visit you," she said.

Finally, the day comes when the doctors tell us I am well enough to be released. This is when I discover I have been in the hospital for nineteen days!

I barely remember the first day I spent in Mississippi and now almost three weeks of my seventeenth year have been lost!

While I can leave the hospital, my mother is advised not to put me on an airplane, and the doctors won't release me to return to school.

It is a good news/bad news proposition.

While I am about to be released from the hospital, my mom can't afford to take any more time off from work; and I am still going to need quite a lot of help. Thankfully, Anne's parents, my Aunt Lora and Uncle Harold, agree to take care of me at their house at the Academy in Northern Mississippi, while I continue to recuperate. Anne was recuperating at home for two weeks after she was released from the hospital but now has returned to school.

I hope I will be ready to return home once Anne finishes her semester at Whitworth College. If so, Anne and I will be able to fly back to Florida together.

Chapter 3

Recovery mode

The trip home from Jackson is long and a little stressful. I am glad to be out of that hospital room; but it is eerie to be riding in a car on The Natchez Trace again, most of it being a tree-lined, two-lane road. I've learned that just before the accident happened, we passed a family, traveling along the same route that Sunday afternoon. When my front tire hit a pothole on the side of the road, and I lost control of the car; their entire family witnessed my car careening off of the road and slamming into a tree. They stopped to help us, and my family learned that the driver of their car had just completed an Emergency Medical Technician course. At first, they all thought Anne was hurt worse than I was because her head was bleeding badly from hitting the dashboard. But while attending to Anne, the driver noticed that I was turning blue—I had hit the steering wheel and stopped breathing. The family was able to get us out of the car, which was quite remarkable, considering I was told that the car was totaled.

The driver gave me mouth to mouth resuscitation and saved my life!

It is agreed that we should stop at the accident sight; I am curious, and my Uncle wants to thank God for watching over us, so we pull over and exit the car.

The tree we hit is heavily damaged, and it is hard to imagine what the scene must have looked like to the people who were helping us or any people who were driving by. It's also difficult to comprehend that Anne and I had come so close to death. My family tells me that Anne informed them that we were planning to switch drivers at River Bend picnic area—just five miles down the road. I was an inexperienced driver, and Anne thought it best that I not drive through Jackson. I wondered, had we changed drivers any earlier, if perhaps *none* of this would have happened.

As I stand across the road from the sign that designates this spot as Milepost 127 and think about our accident, I see something sparkling in the sunlight at the base of the tree.

As I approach, I am surprised to see what is sticking halfway out of the mushy soil—almost covered in pine needles—it is my clear, lucite keychain, with *Sunnie* on it.

When I was in the tenth grade, one of my classmates began calling me Sunnie; because, she said, "I was blonde and always smiling". I liked the nickname and had it added to my first keychain, when I finally got my license, at age seventeen. I can hardly believe nearly three weeks have passed, my keychain is still here; and it has survived this tragedy. It gives me hope; maybe if my special keychain could survive this accident, I will survive it too.

The first few weeks at my Aunt's and Uncle's home don't go so smoothly. After I am released from the hospital, I develop a terrible cough that comes with an excess of mucus that has collected in my lungs. Because my jaw is wired together, it is difficult to expel the phlegm.

I have almost suffocated a couple of times during coughing fits, which is terribly frightening.

Aunt Lora and Uncle Harold, having once worked as missionaries, are trained in several medical procedures. During one particularly bad bout in which I can barely breathe, the two of them debate on whether or not to perform an emergency tracheotomy on me. Several minutes pass with me gasping for air and coughing, and…

Harold prays for me…

Thank God I was able to breathe again—without the emergency procedure.

After that episode—and quite a bit more praying—we persuade the doctors to replace the wires on my jaw plates with rubber bands, so they can easily be broken if something like that happens again. I am now also able to use a straw.

I had lost fifteen pounds while I was in the hospital; and it isn't easy to gain any weight back now, being on a liquid diet. *Strangely enough, I still have a little bit of a belly.*

But since I've spent several weeks, lying in a bed, without any kind of exercise; and as I spend most of my time on the couch now, watching television or napping, I don't worry much about it. I just hope I can get back in shape once I'm able to exercise again.

My Aunt Lora is a wonderful caregiver, and spends a lot of time trying to find creative ways to feed me. She even figured out a way to make a semi-liquid version of "Hamburger Helper". It may sound gross, but when you've gone weeks without eating real food, it is quite a treat.

Someone brought home French fries the other day from the Academy dining hall, and I didn't hesitate to ask for one. All I could do was put it between my lips and taste the salt, but it was so good to me.

When Anne's school semester is over, we have made plans to return to Florida together. Of course, this means a trip back down the Natchez Trace, right past the sight of our accident.

When we do finally make the drive, Uncle Harold pulls the car over at Milepost 127 and says a prayer for the two of us.

This prayer would become a tradition for my Uncle for years to come.

Chapter 4

In the beginning

1960

My name is Eliza Beth; named after my Mother and my Grandmother, kind of. I was born in Arizona, at the end of a very hot summer. I'm sure the last few months of my mother's pregnancy were quite uncomfortable, with Phoenix temperatures steadily above one hundred degrees during those months, and only a swamp cooler and a swimming pool to keep the family cool.

When my parents moved from Ohio to Phoenix in 1958, they started their life in a small apartment with their three-year old daughter, Leigh, spending most warm days in the complex swimming pool. But the apartment was too small for a family of four; so before I arrived, they moved into the two-bedroom house that would become my first home. Leigh had been the only child for almost the first six years of her life, and I was told she was not happy in her new role of big sister. I got a lot of attention—which she was used to getting—because I was born with asthma.

We didn't stay in Phoenix too long after my birth, and I was just about a year and a half old when our family moved back to Ohio.

We were living in the two bedroom house my father had built after having served in the US Army. That same year, my brother, Edward, was born.

There was a small room in between the living room and bedrooms that my father had used as an office; this became Edward's room, and Leigh and I shared a bedroom.

My father had always been a wise investor though; when he purchased the lot on which to build his first house, he also purchased both vacant lots on either side of it. Now that Edward had arrived, our family home was becoming a little too crowded; and at my mother's urging, my father agreed it was time to build a bigger house for all of us. The lot for our new house had a long slope to it, so it was determined a split level house would fit perfectly on the site, and the bottom floor could have a walk out basement.

We sold our little house to a sweet couple with two sons and moved into a rental down the street while construction began on our new home. The younger of the new neighbors' sons, but still four years my senior, would later become one of our babysitters and would influence me with his garage band music and his talent in architectural drawings.

He was also my first official crush.

We moved into our new larger house when I was about five years old.

In the beginning, Leigh and I continued to share a bedroom. But as she became a teenager, she began to complain about that living arrangement, claiming that I was kicking her out of the bed at night. She said she had little privacy, and my early bedtimes required her to be unnecessarily quiet. Once she turned fourteen, having a younger sister around all the time was just too much for her to tolerate.

She convinced our parents that she was old enough to have her own bedroom and was moved into the basement guest room. She would also enjoy the added benefit of having a bathroom all to herself.

Edward and I had always kept all of our toys and board games in the large basement bathroom closet. Leigh felt this bathroom was now her territory and didn't like the idea that we kept *our* belongings in *her* closet and often locked the door to keep us out. Eventually she gave in and let us keep our things on bottom shelves and the floor, while she utilized the upper shelves.

One of our Saturday morning chores was to make sure this bathroom closet was tidy and organized. We weren't allowed to go outside to play until everything was neatly put away.

We spent most of our time in the basement level, watching television, playing games, or doing laundry.

But on Saturday nights the entire family would gather together downstairs and grill steaks and make Jiffy Pop popcorn in our fireplace—built by my grandfather—and watch shows together on our 13-inch television. My parents could have easily afforded a larger television, but they didn't find watching television a necessity and never felt the need to upgrade.

While Leigh's reasons for wanting to move to the basement made sense, I suspected there were others she had kept to herself. My father made sure all the exterior doors were locked before we went to bed each night; but I recall several Saturday mornings, as Leigh got older, going downstairs early to watch television in the *basement family room* and discovering the Arcadia door was now unlocked.

It was obvious to me she spent many nights sneaking out or had friends sneak in after the rest of the family had gone to bed.

Leigh graduated from high school early, at the age of seventeen; she had been a straight A student and head cheerleader at her high school. Leigh had also started modeling at age sixteen and entered her high school beauty pageant her senior year. Although she didn't win the pageant, she won the talent competition and finished as the *runner-up* in the pageant.

She had plans to go to Ohio State University; but those plans changed when Leigh eloped with Bob, her best friend's brother—who was six years her senior.

While the adults sorted out what all of this was going to mean for Leigh's future, Edward and I focused on the fact that we now had the entire basement to ourselves, and I started using the shower in the bathroom downstairs instead of the tub in our bathroom upstairs. It was nice to not have to share a bathroom with my little brother any longer.

By that time, we had also acquired an old piano and I had taken piano lessons on and off for a few years. I also spent hours and hours singing along to my sister's old albums— mostly Carol King. Eventually we also got a portable turntable; and I would play my 45 RPM records in Leigh's old bedroom for hours at a time, singing along to Cher and Karen Carpenter hits. Edward's taste in music leaned more toward Three Dog Night and Chicago songs, and we often listened to those 45's together.

But, our idyllic childhood was brought to a halt when we learned our parents had decided to file for divorce.

No one on either side of the family had ever divorced; this was a big deal, not just for us, but for everyone. While the divorce itself was tragic, things were about to get worse. My mother sat me down on the stairs one afternoon and told me we needed to discuss something.

She told me that we would be moving to Florida to live nearer to her family, my Aunt Lora and Uncle Harold, and my father was going to remain in Ohio.

I threw a fit. My friends and family in Ohio were all I had ever known, having moved there as a toddler and spending the next twelve years of my life there. I cried, and cried, and my mother could do little to comfort me. I went to my room, slammed the door hard and flopped down on my bed and cried some more. Normally, this would have earned me a spanking from my dad, but in this situation, they seemed to understand how difficult this was for me. No matter what anyone said to me about moving, I thought it was the end of the world—at least at first.

Leaving my best friend, Haylie, who I had lived across the street from for most of my life, was the hardest thing.

We had grown up together; danced to American Bandstand and Soul Train together. We took gymnastic and ballet lessons together. We put on plays and fashion shows together; and we learned all the lyrics to her older brothers' rock albums together, the most memorable being "Stairway to Heaven".

She also taught me how to sew the summer before I turned twelve and that would become an important hobby of mine as I grew older.

During our school's spring break, my parents put me and Edward on a plane, with Leigh as our chaperone, to Fort Lauderdale, Florida, to spend time visiting my mother's side of the family.

They had moved to Fort Lauderdale from Chicago the previous year to work in a Christian ministry. Edward and I stayed with Aunt Lora and Uncle Harold and my cousins.

Although we had spent many holidays with them, I took the opportunity to get to know my cousins better. Edward and I spent a lot of our time that week with my cousins, Anne and Lee, swimming in their pool and going to the beach. We also had a younger cousin, Lynn, but she was still a toddler. I loved their house and enjoyed my visit. I fell in love with the sun, the sand, and the ocean and was happy when I realized that I would soon be living near the beach.

At the time, I hadn't thought much about it, but our mom probably had hoped that would be the case when she decided to send us there for our vacation.

While we were in Florida for spring break, my parents had cleaned out our house to prepare it for sale and moved into separate residences.

When we returned from Florida, Edward and I moved in with our mother.

When I returned to school to finish my eighth grade school year, I was actually now excited to move to Florida. Now, I could have a tan all year long, and my friends were jealous. No more walking to the bus stop in the freezing cold winters, with my nose running!

For the remainder of the school year, we temporarily lived in a small, but brand new, two-bedroom condo, which meant Edward got his own room; and I ended up on a twin mattress on the floor in my mother's room.

I was happy we were still close to our old neighborhood, so I could visit Haylie; but I was happier still to find that the complex pool was right outside our front door. I spent every possible moment in that pool or lying out in the sun. I remember having to get my mother's permission to start shaving my legs that summer but only being allowed to shave them just above my knees—though I wasn't told why at the time.

Haylie helped me with this "first time" endeavor.

My father moved into one side of a duplex that had been built by his parents, where he had lived after he was discharged from the Army, before he had built his own house. By this time, my grandfather was deceased and my grandmother was living in an assisted living facility.

I'm sure this was hard on my father—his siblings felt sorry for him; he was the only one in the family to be divorced, and he'd lost his house on top of it. My father was the baby of the family, and all of his siblings were well off and lived in very nice houses in very nice parts of town. His family's gatherings had rarely been held at our house and instead were usually at one of his sibling's homes. This was fine by me; my parents didn't even allow alcohol in our house for parties, but all of his siblings had bars and pool tables and outdoor swimming pools. And we always had a lot of fun at the relatives' houses!

After the school year was over, and the divorce and custody finalized, Aunt Lora and Uncle Harold and my cousins came to Ohio to visit us and discuss moving plans with my mother. Edward had since acquired possession of the portable turntable; and Anne and I were catching up, sitting in his room and listening to her new Elton John album. I decided to take her outside and show her around the complex. When we returned to the condo, our parents gathered us together and said we all *needed to have a talk*.

They had taken the album cover to 'Goodbye Yellow Brick Road' and used a black marker to cross out the titles of the songs we were not allowed to listen to. Additionally, they had gone through the printed lyrics and crossed out any words they deemed unsuitable. I wondered how they expected us to put a record on a turntable but only listen to specific songs.

Our solution to the problem in the future was to only listen to the album when our parents weren't home.

I wondered if this was a foreboding to what life, in Florida, was going to be like. Our upbringing had been strict, attending Church every Sunday and most Wednesday nights, too; and we were raised with good, Christian values. But censoring musical lyrics-with no curse words in them-seemed to be taking things to an entirely new level.

Before the end of the summer, Edward and I moved with our mother from Ohio to Florida.

We lived temporarily with Aunt Lora and Uncle Harold, and my cousins were nice enough to share their bedrooms with us. My mother took on the task of looking for a job and finding us a house of our own.

I was now going to be a Freshman in high school that year, and Edward was going to be in seventh grade. I was closest to my cousin Anne, who was going to be a Junior.

Anne had been going to the public school in their neighborhood, but it had not been a good school; so all of the parents agreed that the three oldest children should instead attend Fort Lauderdale Christian Academy.

It was a private school, a little farther away than the public schools and obviously more expensive since it was a private school; but the parents had determined they would take turns driving us to and from school during the first year, until Anne got her driver's license and a car the following summer.

I'm fairly certain my father paid for most of the tuition for Edward and me, as our mother had just started a job with the City of Fort Lauderdale as a bridge tender and was not making enough money for living expenses and tuition for two to a private school.

While there were more rules to follow at the Christian academy, I was happy to be going somewhere with a smaller student body. I had been a good student but fairly shy and would have been entirely overshadowed at a public school. My brother joined the basketball team, I tried out for and made the cheerleading squad, and Anne was on the yearbook committee.

These activities kept all of us busy after school until one of the parents came to collect us. If we didn't have an activity to do, there was always homework to work on.

I spent much of my spare time with Anne and her friend Ruth, who lived just a few houses away from Anne's house. My Uncle Harold was the pastor of our church, and in time I made friends with some of the kids in the youth group too.

Before the end of the first semester of school, Edward and I and our mother had moved into our own house.

But when Edward finished seventh grade, he decided he wanted to move back to Ohio to live with our dad. He missed all the *father-son* activities the two of them had shared together, like hunting, fishing, and camping.

This was very difficult for my mother, but I also think she thought it would be much easier for her to support only one child instead of two. With the extra space left by my brother's absence, my mother found a renter to move in with us.

Cathy, a single girl from a recovery beach mission where my mom volunteered, was just looking for a temporary place to stay; but her rent money helped cover some of our expenses for most of the next year. Our new roommate also had a sewing machine, and she was happy to lend it to me. Since I had learned how to sew and crochet when I had lived in Ohio, I started making some of my own clothes; so I would have something new to wear once in a while.

Halfway through my sophomore year, I started spending some weekends at my sister's new apartment. Leigh and Bob had divorced after two years of marriage, and she was now single.

Leigh also had a great job with the City of Fort Lauderdale Nursery and was modeling and dating some very successful men, but living alone. She lived in a nicer neighborhood than us, and it was within walking distance of the beach. It just so happened, she was also closer to our private school. Now that Anne had her license, this made it easier for her to pick me up on Mondays.

Some days I would just have my sister drop me off.

Anne and I spent a lot of time at Leigh's apartment before and after high school sports games or other school activities. Leigh allowed us to drink beer at her place. Although it never really agreed with me, I drank it anyway, because that's what everyone else was drinking.

That spring, our mother had asked Leigh to come to church with us for Easter Sunday. I spent the weekend at Leigh's condo and we got up early Sunday to get ready for church.

Although I was fifteen, and my sister now twenty-one, our mother had bought coordinating dresses for the two of us to wear.

On our way to church, Leigh and I were hit head on by an elderly couple driving a Cadillac. Leigh's tiny Volkswagen bug was totaled; but by the grace of God, her newly replaced windshield had not yet set, and it simply popped out upon impact—in once piece.

We were also blessed in that the accident occurred almost directly in front of the Baptist Hospital and paramedics were there within a few minutes. Of course, Leigh and I failed to show up at church, and to this day, I'm still not sure how our mother discovered we had been in an accident.

Leigh and I ended up in the same hospital room; and as this was long before airbags, Leigh hit her chin hard on the steering wheel. The large gash, resulting from the impact, required three layers of stitches—ninety altogether—in an effort to reduce the possibility of a visible scar, since she was still modeling. She was sent to surgery shortly thereafter to repair a broken ankle, caused by her foot getting caught between the pedals while attempting to slam on the brakes.

I'd had my head down, crocheting, while on our way to the church, but just happened to look up in time to see the Cadillac about to hit us. I instinctively threw up my left arm for protection, since there was a crochet hook in my right hand; but my face hit my arm on the dashboard and my wrist was broken upon impact. At first, the doctors were certain I'd broken my nose too. Though I had talked about wanting a nose job in the past, and the doctors thought it might be necessary if my nose was broken; that injury wasn't severe enough to necessitate surgery, but my wrist required two surgeries during that same week.

While Leigh ended up with pins in her ankle, and I ended up with a pin in my wrist; we were endlessly thankful that we had survived a head on collision and were only hospitalized for a week.

During our hospital stay, we exceeded the maximum number of allowable visitors every day. A boy I liked from school, my first official boyfriend, had his mother bring him to visit me; and he brought me activity books to pass the time. It was a sweet gesture; but having already had a tendency toward being self-conscience, I was terribly embarrassed by my appearance.

Because of our injuries, we were both going to need help getting around and doing things; so it was decided I would just move in with Leigh for the rest of the school year and the summer, until we both fully recovered.

I remember how upset I was when my English teacher gave me a failing grade for the semester because I didn't turn in a book report. I had to take my final exams with a bruised face and my left arm in a cast, but I was relieved the school year was coming to an end. Living just minutes from the beach now, that was where I planned to spend my summer.

The arrangement turned out great for me. Eventually, Leigh went back to work, and so each weekday morning I would clean the apartment (my *rent* payment) and then go to the beach; or take her little dog, Huggie Bear, to the dock behind her condo.

When at the dock, I would sit in the sun, watching the boats go by and daydreaming about living at the beach one day. I ended up at the beach most days.

I remember the stares I got as I walked out onto the sand—a skinny teenager in a black bikini, with a large white cast half-way up her bicep. I would awkwardly spread out my beach towel and once I settled into my sunbathing spot, I would *plant* my elbow in the sand while lying in the sun because I didn't want my casted arm to create a tan line across my body. Of course, this caused the elbow section of my cast to get soft from the moisture in the sand; but thankfully, it didn't seem to create any problems. I would wade into the ocean a little to cool off, trying to balance against the current so as not to get my cast wet.

The real fun came when I returned home to shower; trying to secure a large plastic bag over my arm with a rubber band to hold it in place and attempting to shampoo the salt and sand out of my hair with one hand, was not an easy task.

Leigh invited her friends over quite often for drinks and to listen to music. Although all of her friends were much older than I was, Leigh didn't mind if invited my own friends over to join us. Of course, I got away with a lot more living with Leigh than I would have had I been back at home with my mother.

It became a weekend tradition to have parties at her apartment—whether she was there or not. More often than not, she had been spending a lot of time at her new boyfriend's place. None of us really got into serious trouble in those days. It was all fairly innocent—drinking beer, hanging out, watching television or listening to our favorite music.

In the meantime, my mom's renter moved out, and with a monthly payment that was tough for her to afford, and me living with Leigh; my mom decided to move back in with Harold and Lora.

Anne had graduated at the end of the school year, and so toward the end of summer my mom asked me where I wanted to go to high school in the fall, so she could find the two of us an apartment in the school district I chose. I wanted to stay where I was—near the beach, in a nice condo—but that was not an option, not to mention that my sister was not the best person to be supervising a teenager.

I decided I wanted to attend the public high school that two of my friends, June and Terrie, from church, attended—South Plantation High. The school was in a fairly nice, though older, neighborhood; and my mom and I moved into a small apartment within the school district. It was not the ideal area or the nicest apartment in the school district, but my mom had to work two jobs just to afford this apartment and the utilities.

I had my own room and the apartment complex had a pool, so that was all that really mattered to me. I rarely saw other teenagers in the complex, and often wondered if I was the only one living there.

My dad had bought me a bicycle, so I could get around the neighborhood and possibly ride to school; and I kept it locked up on the second floor walkway. To my dismay, it was stolen after just a few weeks. This meant if I wanted to go anywhere, I had to walk or find a ride from friends.

Luckily, after just a few weeks at the school, I became friends with some of the boys that lived in the neighborhood near our complex, and they offered to give me rides to and from school most of my Junior year. Sometimes, my mom would have to drop me off at school, and sometimes I would have to walk home (like when I had to go to summer school the following summer to make up a PE credit and an English credit). Summer PE was fun— playing tennis and pinball at the roller rink—but English vocabulary class, not so much!

I learned how nice the neighborhood between the high school and our apartment was, when I had to walk around the Country Club and Golf Course to get home!

While public schools in Ohio had been quite a bit more challenging, I had returned to a public school in Florida, after two years at a private Christian academy; so all of my classes ended up being very easy for me.

I rarely had any homework and even when I had to write a book report, I only read Cliff notes because I didn't like to read books; I preferred listening to music.

During the week, when I got home from school, I mostly sat outside and designed clothing I wanted to make, or I just hung out by the pool. On the weekends, I hung out at Ruth's house or we went to her friend's houses, since my mother was usually working or volunteering. Most of the time, my mom had to work two jobs to make ends meet. She also volunteered at the recovery beach mission, managed by friends of hers.

Ruth went to a private school down the street from her house, and she had a lot of wealthy friends who were always having parties. Many of the parents would take off for long weekends and leave their kids at home, unsupervised, with enough money to buy whatever they needed. It was so different from my life, and I found it very exciting hanging out with them. Ruth's parents were divorced, and her mom was often out on dates; so we did just about whatever we wanted to on the weekends. Our curfew was one in the morning, but her mom rarely made it home by then herself; so the curfew was not rigidly enforced.

I used to spend a lot of time during the week at home alone, listening to my albums on my portable turntable.

My favorites were Peter Frampton and Heart, but my small stack of albums also included Fleetwood Mac and the Rolling Stones.

When I was at Ruth's house, we mostly listened to Led Zeppelin and the Who; when I was with Leigh, we listened to a lot of Jimmy Buffet and Bob Seger. I liked a lot of different types of music, but mostly Rock and Roll. I also had some friends who volunteered at the beach recovery mission that introduced me to Christian rock—which I liked also.

Every weekday, when it was warm, I was out by the pool when I got home from school or I watched *Guiding Light* on my 13-inch television; and then I would call Ruth. We would talk on the phone until it was time for my mom to come home from work. Every weeknight, I would stay up late and watch "The Tonight Show," but my mom wasn't happy about that because I had to be up by 6 am to get ready for school. I loved listening to Johnny Carson's monologues and was always curious about who his guests would be. From time to time one of my favorite musical groups would perform, and there was no way I was going to miss that.

Whether it was just the nature of our relationship or due to my mom's hectic schedule, we never really formed a close bond. We got along all right, for the most part; but it seemed we rarely said, "I love you."

Chapter 5

Senior year

1977-1978

June and I were in a couple of classes together during our Senior year of high school and started spending more time together. At school, we wandered the halls, singing—June always singing harmonies to my melodies. She had a wonderful voice and could play just about anything on the piano. June also had her license, and a car; and as I had neither, I tagged along with her quite often.

We went together to see Peter Frampton in the Miami Baseball Stadium and ended up setting up our chairs right in front of the stage and the tower of speakers. Of course, this was because it had rained, and the field was mostly mud.

I'd sewn a strapless sundress to wear to the concert, and the two of us must have looked pretty hot because the roadies on stage kept trying to get our attention. Unfortunately, their attempts were a little on the crude side, and I was more embarrassed than flattered. After the concert we were interviewed by a local newspaper, which was very exciting.

I later ended up regretting sitting in front of the speakers because I had ringing in my ears for days afterwards.

One weekend, June's boyfriend, Paul, introduced us to one of his friends, William. The four of us spent the evening at the State Fair, walking around the grounds, talking and people watching.

By the end of the evening, William was holding my hand. I guess they thought we made a cute couple, because we kept ending up together when we went out with June and Paul. I had never really dated much, and my only boyfriend had been the one I had my Sophomore year at the Academy.

He had also been my *first kiss* at age 15.

William and his older brother, George, had quite a few parties at their house throughout the year; and we always attended. William's mom was widowed, and like Ruth's, had a very active social life; she didn't seem to mind who the boys invited over. Their house was beautiful, with a man-made lake out back and lots of land around it. It even had a grand entrance with a moat, and a small bridge over it that led to the front door. Needless to say, I was very impressed with their house. I loved hanging out there. And William? Although my taste leaned more toward the blonde surfer types, he was cute, with awesome curly brown hair and very distinctive features, and he was also very nice to me.

June and I spent a lot of time involved with things related to music. June had played piano most of her life, and she sang and played piano with the school and church choirs.

She decided that perhaps it was time to put together her own band.

One evening we were practicing at her house with some of the school band members, with me on the tambourine and backup vocals. Paul and William showed up to listen; and afterwards, the four of us ended up going over to William's house. The guys were discussing trying to get concert tickets for all of us to go see Led Zeppelin. I was becoming more *impressed* with William every time I saw him.

I also realized that from the outside, people considered us a couple. But I didn't feel that I knew William very well though because we didn't go to the same school and only spent time together in social gatherings.

Later that evening, William received a call from Paul's mom, who was looking for June, because my mother had called June's mom and was looking for me. I then realized June had failed to tell her mom we were leaving with Paul and William. When we went to leave William's house, he stopped and kissed me goodbye for the first time. I was surprised by William's kiss. June and I got into Paul's car, and he drove us back to her house. William had just kissed me for the first time; the evening should have been exciting; but the moment was clouded, as June and her mom argued in the car on the entire drive over from her house to my apartment to drop me off.

I felt as though I was the one that had caused all the trouble, and I felt terrible.

By the time I got home, my mom was so upset with me, she told me I was now grounded for the next two weeks. I begged her to reconsider—my friends and I had tickets to a Bob Seger concert, and they would be so mad at me if I couldn't go. I told my mom if I didn't go, Ruth wouldn't go, and if Ruth didn't go, June wouldn't go; and it would be all my fault. She decided instead to ground me from watching television and spending the weekend at Ruth's house.

It wasn't easy for my mom to inflict punishment on me, knowing that her work schedule meant that I was often alone without much to do.

She worried less about me when I spent the weekends at Ruth's house when she wasn't home much. Sometimes I reflect on the sacrifices my mom made, and I feel remiss in not showing her more appreciation.

After the winter break, I got my driver's license; because I was only going to have three classes my last semester of high school, and I didn't want to have to walk home every day-like I did in Summer school. Most of the time, I took the car and dropped my mom off at work before I went to school; and after school I drove back home and hung out by the pool or watched television and called Ruth until it was time to pick up my mom.

My mom and I would make dinner, and then she would either leave to work her night job or go to help at the recovery beach mission. Sometimes, on weekends, Ruth and I would go with her to the beach recovery mission.

My mom originally had a Pinto, which I had no desire to drive; but later, she traded it in for a Mustang. Although it was a fairly basic model—it didn't even have a radio, but we had a portable cassette player and cassette tapes; I still felt pretty cool driving it to school. As a young girl in Ohio, I'd seen a neighbor driving around the neighborhood in a brand-new Mustang; and I had always imagined having one of my own.

My mom used to allow me to borrow the car on weekends when she was spending a lot of time at the recovery beach mission. Ruth and I loved to drive down the Fort Lauderdale strip and check out the boys on the sidewalk.

We filled the gas tank with our spare change, and my mom never questioned the mileage.

One weekend, in the beginning of February, my mom offered to give a young woman from the recovery beach mission a ride to visit her husband. He was imprisoned in another city in Florida. My mom would be gone for the weekend with her car and left me to stay with Ruth.

June came over to hang out with us at Ruth's house; Ruth's mother was out on a date, but eventually we got bored and decided to go over to my apartment. We stopped at 7-11 and bought some 7-Up on the way. Once at my apartment, June called Paul and suggested he and William come and join us. Shortly thereafter, Leon, whom Ruth had been dating, ended up there as well.

Leon showed up with Canadian Club—which happened to be our favorite 7-Up companion at the time. The group of us sat around the apartment, drinking, talking, and listening to music. This *party* wasn't much different from any other party we'd ever attended, except that it was at *my* apartment, and there were only three couples.

After a while, William and I ended up in my room, on my mattress on the floor, watching television. As teenagers sometimes do, we eventually started kissing. Our privacy didn't last too long though, as soon thereafter, Ruth knocked on my door and asked to borrow something out of my dresser. That was when I heard more voices in the living room and decided I better see what was happening.

I remember thinking that Ruth's interruption was probably good timing anyway, as things had been heating up a little between William and me.

When I stepped into the living room, there were four more boys standing in it. The group of them played in a band of some sort. Ruth had invited them to come over and join us.

I'd had enough to drink that I didn't really care that there were now ten people in our tiny, 2 bedroom—1 bathroom apartment.

June and Ruth approached me and were startled by the hickeys on my neck. While they reminded me that our moms would not be happy if they saw something like that, I told them not to worry; I was sure they would fade quickly.

I had never had hickeys before and was quite naïve.

We continued hanging out in the living room, listening to music; but soon afterwards, the band guys left, most likely not interested in hanging out with three couples.

We all had the sense to realize none of us was in any position to drive anywhere. Everyone called their parents, claimed they were sleeping over at one or the other's houses; and we all stayed the night at my apartment.

It got to be pretty late and William and I ended up back in my bedroom, Paul and June ended up in my mom's room, Leon and Ruth ended up on the floor of the living room. I must have passed out pretty quickly when we all finally decided to go to bed, because I don't remember a lot about the rest of the night/morning. Though, I do remember making out with William, his body next to mine, and *almost* having sex.

When I awoke that morning with William in my bed, I was surprisingly totally naked!

I was embarrassed—I was always somewhat shy, and this was the first time I had ever woken up in bed, next to a guy —and naked. I grabbed my robe and immediately went to the bathroom.

I looked into the mirror and saw that my mascara was smeared, my hair was a mess, and there were still hickeys all over my neck. It was pretty clear to me why Ruth and June had been so concerned about them the night before— how was I going to hide these from everyone? I peed, brushed my hair, brushed my teeth, and washed my face.

I didn't normally wear much make up, but I found some of my mom's foundation in the cabinet and tried to cover the marks on my neck; but it was too dark for me, so I washed it off!

"Hey some of us need the restroom too," it was Ruth and June, who were also now awake and knocking on the bathroom door. I returned to my bedroom to get some clothes and get dressed, and by now, everyone else was up and in the living room, ready to take their own turns in the bathroom.

Ruth and June followed me into my bedroom and wanted to know what had happened between me and William.

I knew that no one else there really cared if William and I had had sex, but clearly the girls were curious to know the details. I told them we had made out, fallen asleep—and while we came close to having sex, we never really had intercourse.

I had NOT lost my virginity—I was stating the truth.

I was certain that even though we were pretty wasted the night before, and my memory wasn't fully accurate; I would have felt *different* if something like that had happened between us. I couldn't deny that my initial appearance that morning might have implied otherwise; but I was sure I would have known if our *almost* having sex had been *actually* having sex, and I had just lost my virginity. With that said, there was no way I was going to ask William.

Ruth and June were still concerned about my neck but said they would try to help me cover it more thoroughly after the guys left. I just hoped the hickeys would fade quickly —my mom wouldn't be home for another day or so, but Ruth's mom would be home when we got back to her house. I did my best not to worry about it while we all cleaned up the apartment and got all of our stories straight on who stayed where. After the boys said their goodbyes, the three of us piled into the bathroom in an effort to properly camouflage the hickeys.

As June drove us back to Ruth's house, the two of them kept asking me what really happened with William. I kept trying to explain things to them, without providing intimate details. To me, my intact virginity seemed like the most important point. "We came close," I told them, "but, you know, we were pretty drunk, and...at one point, even if I had wanted to, it was pretty clear that it couldn't happen... if you know what I mean."

I was only seventeen and seven months away from turning eighteen and in no hurry to lose my virginity really.

And I wasn't planning on loosing my virginity to someone I hadn't known that long or that well and did not feel I was in love with.

William was almost a year younger than I was, and I didn't know if he was experienced or not. But, all the alcohol was obviously a little too much for both of us.

When I got my period a couple of weeks later, I joked around with Ruth again about nothing really happening, but told her maybe I should think about going on the pill—just in case something did happen in the future.

Over the next few weeks, we went to a couple of parties at William's house, but things were different between us. He didn't behave as though he was my boyfriend, and we didn't make out again. Although we still seemed like friends, we didn't seem like a couple anymore.

I wasn't sure what to do or say and wondered if maybe he was just as embarrassed (or confused) about the whole thing as I was.

My concerns about my relationship—or lack thereof—with William were quickly a thing of the past when I learned that June was being sent away to finish our senior year of high school out of state. I was devastated. With only a few months left in the semester, I wondered if her parents were trying to separate her from Paul. June and Paul had been together since the eighth grade, but somehow I felt as though this all was my fault—again. I worried all of the parents had started talking and comparing stories and realized everyone had lied about where we were the night they slept at my apartment. I didn't know what I was going to do if my mom found out that everyone had stayed overnight at our place.

June was sent to a Christian academy in Northern Mississippi where my Aunt Lora and Uncle Harold were now working. I missed her terribly, but at least I still had Ruth. I went to a few parties with Ruth and some of her other friends during the next few weeks, but we no longer went to William's house since June was gone and we no longer hung out with her and Paul. When my mom asked me if I wanted to drive up to Northern Mississippi with her for my spring break and the Easter Holiday to visit her family—and June—I was beyond excited.

I didn't realize it at the time, but my mom had other reasons for wanting to visit our Mississippi relatives. We'd moved to Florida after my parent's divorce to be nearer to her family, and now that Lora and Harold had moved to Mississippi, my mom was considering moving us there, too. I think my mom was hoping I would enjoy our time there, as I had in Florida in high school, and be less inclined to object to such a move.

I had previously told my mom that I wanted to do lifeguard training on the Fort Lauderdale Beach or go to The Art Institute of Fort Lauderdale for Fashion Design after I graduated, but my mother didn't seem to be happy about either of my choices. Ruth and I had even talked about going to Florida State University together.

My mom took me out of school early that week so we could get to Northern Mississippi before the Holiday weekend.

We arrived on the Thursday evening before Palm Sunday. My cousin, Anne, had not returned home from college in Southern Mississippi yet but would be arriving on Friday afternoon for the weekend.

I went to visit June in her dorm and was invited by her to go with the Academy's choir to a competition at Mississippi State University the next day. The choir teacher ok'd me to go with them since our family worked at the Academy.

I don't remember much about that weekend, but I really loved spending time with June again, sharing stories with her dorm mates about all the trouble we used to get into. I got the feeling my mom and Aunt Lora thought we would end up spending too much time together and so made other plans for me during the week we were in Mississippi.

They asked Anne to take me back to college with her for the week. She planned to return to Northern Mississippi on Good Friday, just in time for the Easter weekend. After the Palm Sunday service at the church, the family all had lunch together in the Academy's dining hall.

I was told it was a slightly overcast day and had sprinkled a little, but it must have still been quite warm because I changed into my jeans and a no sleeved light pink shirt I had made.

If Anne and I were still in Florida, we would have probably been headed to the beach for an afternoon in the sun. Instead, we left shortly after lunch for our three-hour drive to Whitworth College.

Chapter 6

Back to the beach

After being released from the hospital, I ended up spending over two months in Northern Mississippi, recovering from our car accident. When Anne and I landed back in Fort Lauderdale, the first trip we made, after getting back to our apartment, was to the beach. It felt great to be around friends and familiar faces again. Ruth and I were so happy to see each other again.

She told me she was so afraid she had lost me—the day of the accident, she felt deeply that something was terribly wrong. When our friend, Cathy, who was staying in our apartment while we were in Mississippi, called her; she burst into tears, thinking the worst.

June had graduated from the Academy and returned home. It's no surprise she and Paul had picked up their relationship right where they left it, which made me even more confused as to why she had to leave Fort Lauderdale in the first place.

No one thought to withdraw me from school after the accident, and I found out I had been given failing grades for the last eight weeks of high school.

I was fortunate in that I was only taking three classes during my last semester and receiving A grades in all them, so the Principal agreed to let me go ahead and take my final exams, using my textbooks; so I didn't have to go to summer school, again.

The accident caused me to miss my senior prom, the annual graduation celebration at Disney World, and my graduation ceremony. Though I didn't have a date for the prom, I remember hoping a particular blonde surfer boy that I had been flirting with in the hallways, was going to ask me to the prom. I'd already picked out a pattern for the dress that I was going to make. I was also especially sad to miss the trip to Disney World; during those celebration nights, the entire park was closed to the public and only graduating high school seniors were allowed inside. While I was thankful to get a diploma and my graduation tassel, I wished I could have formally graduated with the five hundred other seniors in my class.

During my first month back home, I spent a lot of time at the beach. I'd barely gained a pound, because I was still on a liquid diet; but I was annoyed that my stomach still was not flat. I tried to exercise, but it just made me dizzy. I had been given an MRI before I was released from the hospital, so that my doctors could make sure I had no permanent brain damage, I assumed. So far, vertigo seemed to be the only side effect of my head injury.

My mom had scheduled an appointment with my ENT doctor so I could have the jaw plates and wires removed and start eating solid foods again. I never imagined the day would come that I would be tired of chocolate milk shakes. The doctor was concerned the jaw plates had kept my mouth in a closed position for so long and was more than happy to remove them. He warned me that it may take a while to get used to chewing solid foods again. Of course, I ignored his warning and went out with June, Paul and Ruth for a steak dinner right away. It was difficult to chew but was probably the most delicious steak I'd ever had!

One day, out of the blue, my mom asked me if I'd had my period since the accident. The doctors had told her I might be out of synch for a while—between the coma, the surgery, the medications, and the restricted diet.

I hadn't really thought much about it but didn't recall having my period in the hospital. The more I thought about it, I never had it while I was in Mississippi recovering either, and I hadn't had one since I'd been back to Florida.

My mother suggested taking me to a gynecologist to make sure everything was okay. I'd never been to a gynecologist before, and I wasn't looking forward to it. But after being in the hospital for nearly three weeks, poked and prodded, while wearing only a thin hospital gown; I wasn't as shy as I'd been before.

After a routine examination (I assumed) and a lot of
questions, the doctor instructed me to get dressed and then
come to his office.

While poised in his over-sized leather office chair, seated
behind his gigantic maple desk, he told me that everything
looked healthy and normal.

"Why did you tell me you were still a virgin," he asked?

"I am still a virgin. I have never had sex," I replied.

He explained that the only reason he could find that I
hadn't had my period recently was because…

I was between twelve and sixteen weeks pregnant!

For a moment, I felt like I just careened off of the road
again, into another tree.

I explained to him that I had not had sexual intercourse, and
I tried to explain my *encounter* with William.

"And that was in February?" he asked. Then he looked at
me suspiciously and asked again when my car had accident
had occurred.

"The accident was in March, on Palm Sunday, and I had
my period two weeks after…two weeks after…William.
But we did not have sexual intercourse. How could this
have happened?" I asked.

Perhaps it seemed like a dumb question, but I really did consider myself a virgin still.

The doctor explained that it was unlikely, but possible, that a pregnancy could occur in the situation I described, *close enough* but no actual intercourse. "But it's rare. Maybe one in one hundred thousand," he told me.

I'd always wanted to be special—different in some way, unique; but this was not what I had in mind!

Whatever further conversation we had that followed escapes my memory; because by that time, shock had set in. I do, however, recall his condescending tone; and it was obvious he didn't think I was telling him the truth.

He kept pressing me to tell him whether I had any other encounters with William, or anyone else. I told him again that it had been the one and only *sexual encounter* I had ever had and was certain it occurred in February, several weeks before my car accident. He must have mistaken my shock for hesitation, because it was clear he thought I was trying to lie.

The fact was, my brain could barely comprehend what he was telling me.

"Would you like me to share my findings with your mother, or would you like to tell her yourself?" I wanted to tell her myself, but I wondered how on earth I could do it.

In the past, I would gone running to Ruth or to Leigh with news like this, but my mom had been by my side through everything—the accident, the recovery—and she was going to have to be told.

I said I wanted him to do it, and so he invited her into the room. I just sat, frozen in the chair, staring past him, out the window.

Needless to say, she was as shocked as I was. She asked me when and where this had happened. I told her what I had told the doctor, but we quickly agreed this discussion should be continued after our appointment had concluded. Wanting to avoid getting into the middle of a family situation, the doctor changed the subject.

"Well, the next question we have to answer is, what do we do now?"

We went over my recent medical history—again.

He told us that because of my car accident and being without oxygen possibly, and having a head injury, ending up in a coma, having surgery, and probably being given a long list of medications; he would suggest an abortion.

"Being that no one in the hospital ever knew you were pregnant, they would not have taken any precautions to protect the fetus and there is no way to really know what kind of harm may have been caused".

He had me scared all right, but I was also surprised. I'd known of a couple of girls who'd had abortions. "But I thought you could only have an abortion up to twelve weeks of pregnancy?" I replied.

My mom looked at me, surprised; I didn't acknowledge her stare.

He told us that for *medical reasons* he could recommend an abortion up to twenty weeks. He reminded us we had little time to decide what to do if I had actually conceived in the beginning of February, as I was most likely already sixteen weeks into my pregnancy.

We told him we would discuss my options, and let him know once we'd made a decision.

My mom and I left his office and sat in her *new* Chevy Impala in the parking lot for a long while. I tried to explain everything the best that I could. This was really difficult since my mom and I had never really discussed sex. I had learned most of what I knew from my friends or from school sex education classes. Of course, she was hurt because she had always trusted me not to get into trouble. At one point she blamed much of it on my two best friends, claiming they were bad influences; but I told her it was my fault, not theirs.

And it had only happened that one time.

My mom asked me who *the boy* was, but I did not tell her his name. I said she'd never met him, and he was a friend of Paul's I'd met the previous year. She wanted to know if he was the boy who had visited me in the hospital, I told her, "No". I explained to her that we were no longer seeing each other, so she had no reason to meet him.

My mom and I had never really even talked about boys and dating, and I wasn't about to start now. The conversation was becoming increasingly upsetting, and I told her the stress was causing me heartburn. She didn't want to upset me any further, and so she drove us back to our apartment.

I rode in the car, silent, realizing that my world had just been turned upside down; and all my future plans—staying in Florida, hanging out at the beach, perhaps even going to college—had just changed. I was pregnant. This baby was now my number one priority—even though this doctor, a medical specialist, had just suggested I have an abortion.

I was so confused. My brain was still not functioning at one hundred percent; and now, not only was I trying to decide what to do with my life, I was trying to make decisions about my baby's life, too. I had just been told I was carrying a child that could be mentally or physically disabled because of what we had been through. I didn't know what to do.

My mom suggested I pray about it.

The truth was, I had never felt like God really answered prayers. To me, it seemed prayer just helped me concentrate more on a situation in order to make up my own mind—more like meditation. But now, I needed a sign; I needed to feel that there was nothing wrong with this baby in order for me to consider going through with this pregnancy.

We decided not to tell anyone at first, since we weren't sure what I was going to do. But soon, my mom ended up telling her best friend, Karen, at the recovery beach mission. In time, my dad and sister were also told.

Everyone had their own opinions of what I should do, but it was my decision to make, so I told them I was considering all my options. I did not tell any of my friends because I didn't want this to get back to William.

Karen gave my mom a pamphlet on abortion to pass along to me. It was one of those "When Does Life Begin?" type of things.

In the past, having an abortion in the event of an unplanned pregnancy was something I had thought would be a pretty easy decision to make, knowing of others who had had abortions. But, being faced with the reality of having to make such a decision now was not so simple.

I knew a pamphlet couldn't explain what I should do in my current situation, since I had been told something could be wrong with the baby I was carrying; but I decided to read it anyway. Sitting on my mattress on the floor, pamphlet in hand, I prayed for God to give me some sort of sign to help me decide what to do.

And then, something unexpected happened...

I felt a flutter in my belly!

I sat, frozen, wondering if it was real—and then, it happened again. A very distinct flutter.

This baby was letting me know it was real.

I jumped up and ran into my mom's room and told her to feel my belly, explaining to her what had just happened. She felt it too and smiled—probably for the first time in weeks.

"I'm not going to have an abortion!" I said. "I don't know what I'm going to do, but I can't purposely kill a baby that God has protected through everything that's happened to us!"

Just because one doctor said I should have an abortion—a doctor who did not really know me or my entire story—didn't mean I had to let him have the final say in my decision.

Thankfully, my mom found another doctor we could discuss this with and he requested my medical records from the hospital in Mississippi and had a rush put on them. He scheduled an appointment with us as soon as they arrived. This doctor was very understanding and not judgmental at all.

We discussed everything that had happened to me while he reviewed my medical records and pages of medications I had been given during my hospital stay. We went over every procedure, every medication. His opinion was much different from that of the first doctor.

He told me and my mom that he did not see anything that happened that would put a fetus at any more risk than a normal pregnancy. He explained to us since I was not without oxygen long enough to cause me any brain damage, the fetus would not be affected by that—as it was not breathing oxygen yet anyway. According to all of his tests, it seemed I was doing just fine and so was my baby.

I explained to him also that this pregnancy had come about from one *encounter* with a boy I was seeing at that time, and he said that though there was a very small chance, it was obviously possible to get pregnant in this situation. He also pointed out that since I knew the exact date of conception, it would be easy to predict my due date.

He then asked me if I was interested in a home for unwed mothers; I told him I did not yet know for sure what I was going to do about my living arrangement.

It seemed destined that I would be moving to Mississippi with my mom after all. I would have time to decide what I was going to do about my future—and my baby's—beyond that. My mom had intended on relocating to Northern Mississippi at the end of the school year, but my accident had delayed her move. I'm not sure what she thought I would do, being unemployed and only seventeen at the time. I guess she was always praying that I would want to move with her by the time I had visited Mississippi and graduated from high school.

Now that I had my high school diploma, I decided I would move with my mom, temporarily, until I was well enough to work and support myself. But now, I had more decisions to make. I still wasn't sure if I should keep and raise a child on my own or put my baby up for adoption.

But the thought of just giving my baby away to a total stranger to raise, was something I knew I couldn't do.

I told Ruth that I would be moving away with my mom, and I had to tell her why. She was devastated. I begged her not to tell June, because I knew June would tell Paul; and Paul would tell William.

As we were no longer a couple and hadn't even seen each other or talked since before my trip to Mississippi, I did not want him or his family involved in any of my decisions.

Ruth felt like she was losing me all over again. She had just started getting used to me being back in Florida and now, I was leaving and moving to Mississippi.

Ruth wasn't the only one that was torn apart over this; I had imagined so many possibilities in our future—together—and most of them in Fort Lauderdale, where it was sunny and warm and my beloved beach was just a short drive away.

Before we moved, my mom's friends at the recovery beach mission gave us a going away party, and a group of my friends and I went to see one last concert together.

I wasn't sure I wanted to go to the concert, since there would be so many people there. But I looked like any other female high school teen graduate—permed hair in spiral curls (just like Peter Frampton's), dressed in a white cotton sundress, with a summer tan.

I couldn't have hidden my growing belly at the beach any longer; but in my sundress, no one suspected anything. Ruth was the only person at the concert who knew about my pregnancy.

She was so protective, making sure no one got close enough to bump into me, telling them she didn't want them to hurt me because I was still recovering from my car accident.

It just so happened we also ran into William at the concert…

Over thirty-thousand people at an outdoor concert, and we run into the one person I wasn't planning on seeing again. He was surprised to see me there; he told me he had last heard I was still recovering from my car accident in Mississippi.

I held my stomach in and tried to be cool, but I wondered if he still had any feelings for me? I didn't ask, and he didn't say.

Ruth on the other hand, told me later that she wanted to punch him. She felt like it was his fault I was moving away.

Chapter 7

Moving again

My mom and I packed up our furniture and shipped the few things we had to Lora's and Harold's house. Our personal belongings were packed and loaded into my mom's Impala. It was an eighteen-hour drive to Northern Mississippi. We had done this drive just months before, but this time it was different; I wasn't excited to go see family or friends; I was leaving Florida, my beach, and my family and friends who still lived there.

We stayed in a hotel the first night. It was July, hot and humid, and with a couple hours of daylight remaining; we decided to take advantage of the hotel's swimming pool. My bikini days were clearly behind me for now; my mom had bought a maternity swimsuit for me to wear. It had orange and yellow flowers on it, with big bottoms and a long top. It was a far cry from the little, black bikini I was accustomed to wearing; but as far as maternity swimsuits went, it wasn't *too bad.*

A woman, who was swimming in the pool with her children, took up a conversation with my mom.

She looked over at me, sitting on the stairs, and asked if my husband was also in the military and inquired as to where he might be stationed. I didn't say a word. *Why do you assume I'm married?* (*I*s what I wanted to say to her.)

But the realization of how pregnant I now looked, and the reality of my situation, was really beginning to sink in.

I had to acknowledge just how hard it was going to be having a baby on my own. My mom carried on the conversation without really answering her question probably; and I slipped back into the pool and swam away from them, daydreaming about my future.

If I had been a self conscience teenager in the past, my anxiety then had been nothing compared to now-with the stares and judgments I saw in people's eyes. Walking through the world as a pregnant teen drew attention everywhere I went and the obvious assumption that I had been promiscuous. While people were questioning my character, it was just too complicated to even try to explain. But sometimes it made me angry; was I the first pregnant teenager anyone had ever seen? Were they all hidden away in homes for unwed mothers?

Did adults not realize that a lot of single teenagers were not virgins?

Were all of the parents that naive or did they just not want to think about it?

As the weeks went on, being out in public became more and more stressful. My mom and I had settled into Lora and Harold's place. Anne and I were sharing a room this time around (since she was home for the summer), but it was very strange. We weren't the same two people we were before the car accident. It was hard to believe so much had happened in the past four months. I was thankful my mom hadn't sent me to live in some group home; she must have known I couldn't have handled it mentally.

But our stay with family didn't last very long; Lora, Harold and my mother had determined that Northern Mississippi wasn't the best place for me. My Aunt and Uncle were employed at a Christian Academy there, and being that I was pregnant and unmarried, it was just too scandalous for small town Mississippi.

My Uncle knew of a family in Southern Mississippi, where Anne had been attending college, with whom my mom and I could live temporarily. They were wonderfully kind people; opening up their home to us, keeping us both well-fed, and me entertained with magazines and puzzles to pass the time.

My mom found a job as a waitress at a local hotel restaurant, which enabled us to move into our own apartment for a few months. Whitworth College was within walking distance; so, once the semester started, I began taking night classes in Accounting twice a week.

I knew this endeavor was going to be difficult—I could already tell that my reading and learning skills had diminished after my head injury. I had difficulty concentrating and understanding what I was reading, but the doctors had suggested this was the best thing for me to do. This also gave me something more to do than just sit around the apartment, listening to music on my new stereo (my one big purchase with my settlement money from Leigh's and my car accident), talking to my unborn baby, and trying to decide what I was going to do in the future.

I knew my mom disliked her job and wanted to return to Northern Mississippi to work with our family at the Academy, but there was no way she was going to leave me alone. It wasn't just my pregnancy—no matter how disappointed she had been with my choices, having almost lost me in a car accident had been terribly frightening.

I had so many decisions to make.

I still had most of the money left in the bank from my settlement, though I had loaned some of it to my mom to help with our move; perhaps, I thought, I could use the cash I still had to move back to Florida and find a job. But living in Florida wasn't cheap; and I still wasn't driving, let alone in possession of a car of my own. Also, I wasn't sure if I should keep my baby and try to raise it by myself or take a serious look at adoption. I asked my baby all the time what he or she wanted me to do.

We had been through so much together—I began to wonder if perhaps God would be willing to give me another sign.

So, I prayed and asked God if He would give me another sign…and I waited…

By the time we moved to Southern Mississippi, we had located an Obstetrician in Jackson; and my mom was taking me to his office for my appointments every two weeks. We had to drive about an hour each way to see him, but I really liked him. He never once seemed to cast judgment on me. As the weeks rolled on, he even became somewhat of a father figure to me.

During one particular visit, my doctor came right out and asked me if I had decided what I was going to do with my baby. In fact, he specifically asked if I was planning to keep it or give it up for adoption. I told him I still hadn't decided, but I felt as though I couldn't just give my baby to total strangers to raise. If I gave up my baby, I wanted it to be raised in a loving, Christian home, by a couple who would be open about the adoption—a family who was involved in their church and loved music and would treat my baby like the miracle he or she was.

I wanted to give my baby a chance to do whatever he or she wanted to do in life, and I didn't feel like I could give my baby many options. I was single, unemployed and not quite eighteen yet, and I was having a hard time just trying to figure out what to do with my own life.

To my surprise, my doctor gave me a curious smile. He revealed to me something that would have been a violation of numerous privacy statutes today, but at the time was information that seemed to be—once again—a part of God's plan.

He shared with me that he had a patient who had suffered several miscarriages, and she and her husband were now on a five-year waiting list to adopt a baby. "The wife has given notice at her school, and told them she won't be back to teach in the fall," he shared. "She told them she and her husband have been praying for a baby, and God has told her He would bring them one," he continued.

I was trying to take this all in.

My doctor asked me if he could tell this couple about my baby and a little about me. He thought it was a Godsend that I would show up here, in his office, in Jackson, from Florida—by way of Northern and Southern Mississippi.

He said if I was comfortable with the idea, he would talk with them about me and my baby and maybe have their lawyer contact me about the possibility of them adopting my baby.

I could not believe it. Perhaps God was, once again, answering my prayers.

I'd always heard, "With faith, all things are possible." Proof of this seemed to be manifesting itself all around me.

I told my doctor, "Yes," he could share my information with this couple.

The strongest sense of peace came over me after that appointment. I was not giving up on my baby—I was giving it a future. I told my mom that I had made up my mind, this was what I wanted to do.

I knew my mom would have helped me had I chose to raise my baby on my own, but I had to acknowledge that doing so would be a long, hard road—for both of us. I also knew how much she still wanted to return to the Academy to work with her family. I was almost eighteen now, and the final decision was mine to make. I felt in my heart that this was the right thing to do.

How could I ignore these obvious answered prayers?

Soon afterwards, we were contacted by a lawyer and scheduled a meeting with him when we were going to my next doctor appointment. I remember the smile on my doctor's face when I told him we were meeting with the adoptive couple's lawyer later that day.

The lawyer was also very kind and gave us a little more information about the couple who were interested in adopting my baby.

He gave us far more information than would typically be appropriate, but the couple had given him the go-ahead in an effort to assure me they were the right parents for my child. He told me that they were very involved with their church, sang in the choir, and were both school teachers.

He also advised me that the couple would be covering all of the medical bills associated with the baby, which was an additional source of relief. I assumed my dad's insurance had been covering all of my medical bills so far, but I wasn't sure who would cover the baby's bills once he or she was born. The lawyer asked if he could share with them a little more information about me, as well.

And then he asked if I knew who the baby's biological father was. I wasn't expecting this question and was shocked to consider the implications of answering it.

But I had to be truthful and told him, "Yes, I definitely knew the identity of the father".

He told me he was required by law to get a release from the biological father before the adoption paperwork could be completed. This was another surprise, and something I had not been prepared for. I explained that I had not told the biological father I was pregnant before I moved away from Florida, and we had only been *intimate* once. I explained that since we were no longer together when I learned of the pregnancy, I was afraid of the trouble it might cause to everyone involved.

The lawyer told me if I didn't include the biological father's name on the adoption paperwork, the father would be listed as unknown. This meant that if the child wanted to find his or her real parents in the future, it would make it difficult to impossible to learn the identity of the father. This would make it even harder at times to find the mother, especially if her last name had changed.

It might also make me look promiscuous.

I didn't want my baby growing up and possibly finding out from his or her adoptive parents that the biological mother didn't know who the biological father was. I also didn't want to take any options of finding us in the future away from our baby and told the lawyer as much.

The lawyer instructed me to write a letter to the biological father, explaining everything to him in writing; and he would send my letter along with the legal documents.

I explained to him that William was not yet eighteen, and asked if this was going to create a problem with the adoption paperwork.

He told me that in this particular situation, William would be considered a legal adult.

Once these documents were signed by both of us, they would give custody to the adoptive parents.

The lawyer informed me that I would be signing the final document after I gave birth to the baby, as I would still have three days to change my mind.

I was terrified.

Was William going to be angry with me for keeping this information from him? Would he remember seeing me at the concert, realizing I had known and said nothing to him? I hoped, knowing we had not remained in a relationship, that he would understand my reasoning.

About four weeks later we were back at the lawyer's office to complete more of the adoption paperwork. He handed me an envelope, addressed to me, which contained a letter from William. I was afraid to read it but relieved to discover he wasn't mad at me and was, in fact, apologetic. He was thankful that I had taken care of all of this on my own.

At the time, I figured it was because he didn't have to share this information with his family.

I shared my letter with my mom and the lawyer, who asked if he could share it with the adoptive parents.

Sadly, my letter never found its way back to me.

Chapter 8

New life

My baby's due date was the 27th of October. My mom and I went about our day as usual, and we ran errands together after she got off work. I remember a bank teller asking me when I was due, and I told her "Today!" She looked at me like I was a little crazy; but the fact was, other than some mild back discomfort, I felt fine. But by the time my mom and I returned home, I began to have back spasms; so my mom called the doctor's office.

The nurse told my mom I was probably having "back labor" and when my contractions were about five minutes apart, we should head to the hospital. Unfortunately, the hospital happened to be an hour's drive away. As my contractions already seemed to be nearing the five-minutes-apart mark, we decided we should leave right then. Because my mom was so nervous about driving and trying to pay attention to me while I was in labor, she asked our friend, Pam, if she would come along and drive our car to Jackson.

When we got to the hospital, I was taken directly into a labor room. I was checked by a nurse who told me I was dilating, and she would contact my doctor.

When she came back into the room a short time later to *prep* me for delivery, she discovered there was no time for prep and took me directly to the delivery room. My doctor arrived shortly thereafter, and I was set up with an IV.

I hadn't asked for medication of any kind, but I was given an injection in my back and became numb from the waist down almost immediately. After that, I was instructed to push. It all happened incredibly fast. Within a matter of minutes, my baby came into the world.

"It's a girl!" I heard someway say.

And then, another voice, "Shhh . . . she isn't keeping her."

I was groggy from whatever they had put in my IV and only saw the back of the nurse as she carried my little girl out of the room. After all of the post-birth procedures were completed, I was taken to a private room. Sometime later another young nurse came in to check on me. She didn't seem to know I had just had a baby and talked as though I was quite young to be having surgery.

How did she not know I'd just had a baby?

I didn't say a word.

How was I supposed to explain to a stranger that I had just had a baby girl, but I would never be able to hold her, feed her, or comfort her when she cried?

My mom and Pam stopped by my room to say goodbye, and my mom said she'd come back to see me the next day. I found out from them that I had been moved to the women's surgical ward and out of labor and delivery.

That explained why the nurse who had come in earlier had just assumed I'd had some other female related surgery and had no idea I'd just given birth.

I just stayed in bed and watched television to help take my mind off my current circumstances. I was brought something to eat, which I nibbled on. I watched television the remainder of the evening, and I fought back my tears.

Finally, exhausted, I closed my eyes and fell asleep.

The next day, Saturday, my mom brought me some clean clothes to wear home from the hospital the following day and some magazines to read. She told me she stopped by the nursery to see the baby; she just wanted to make sure everything was okay and that the baby was healthy.

"I know the baby is a girl, mom. I heard one of the nurses say so."

"She has dark hair—a lot of it—I think she takes after her grandmother," she told me. I reminded her of William's ancestry, and she agreed that perhaps it came from his side of the family. "Maybe it comes from both sides of the family." I added.

We hung out in my room and watched something on the television for a while, we didn't talk much. "Are you ok? Do you plan on going by the nursery to see her too?" she asked. "I feel like its best if I don't see her. I am content in knowing that she is healthy." I replied.

I really hadn't decided if I wanted to see her or not. I assumed that if I saw what she looked like, it would forever be etched in my mind and that may make giving her up even harder.

My mom told me she couldn't stay long, she had to leave to go to work but would be back the next afternoon, after church, to take me home from the hospital.

Alone in the hospital room, I began to consider what my lawyer had told me about the three day period following the birth, which gave me the right to rescind the adoption agreement. It had been less than twenty-four hours. There was still time for me to change my mind. But if I did, who would pay the hospital bill? Where would we live, how would I support myself and a baby too, and who would I trust to care for my baby while I worked?

And if I did decide to keep her, who would tell the adoptive parents I had changed my mind?

Later that afternoon, a nurse told me I could get up and walk around; so I put on a robe and wandered out into the hallway. There were signs with arrows on the wall, one of them pointing in the direction of the nursery. Was I allowed to go there and look at the babies? I decided to go the opposite way and walked down a different hallway, thinking I would go by the nursery on my way back around. But I just couldn't do it. I had so many doubts, but I knew they were not justified.

I also realized seeing my baby girl now would definitely make giving her up much harder.

I returned to my room, climbed into bed, and tears ran down my cheeks. More than sadness, I felt a deep loss inside of me. After so many months of carrying her, feeling her kick and move around inside of me, and talking to her; the thought that something was missing was ever present. I started thinking about my future and what I was going to do —now that I was eighteen—now that it was just *my* future I had to worry about.

The next morning, I woke after a restless sleep, ate my breakfast, and got myself dressed. I waited for my mom's arrival. It was still too early for my mom to pick me up, so I hung out on my bed, watching television shows. I was surprised by a knock at my door. A nurse entered the room with a young man and a woman, both were dressed professionally; the man carrying a briefcase.

They introduced themselves as assistants to the lawyer. They told me they were there, so I could sign off on the final adoption paperwork. They explained to me that the couple adopting my baby would be taking him or her home from the hospital the following afternoon.

The lawyer's assistants asked me if everything was okay, if I had any doubts, and if I still wanted to sign the papers.

They then explained that even though it had only been less than forty-eight hours since I gave birth, since I would be released from the hospital before seventy-two hours; they were having the paperwork signed before I left. The baby would stay in the nursery until Monday afternoon, when the adoptive parents would take him or her home. I didn't bother to tell them I knew the baby was a girl—it didn't matter. It felt far too late to turn back now, and so I told them everything was fine. I took the pen they extended to me and signed my signature to the paper.

This was the first, and probably most important, legal document I would sign as an adult.

They walked out of the room with the briefcase, again, in the man's hand. I felt alone and depressed and wondered if I should go try to see *my* baby—before it was too late.

My heart was beating as I stepped out into the hallway.

I looked at the sign, looked toward the nursery, and wondered what would happen if the adoptive parents were here now, and I ran into them? What would I say? Legally, I may have had another twenty-four hours to change my mind, but the papers had been signed and technically, the baby was theirs.

I returned to my room and turned on the television again to distract me. When my mom arrived, a nurse came into the room with her to give me my discharge papers, along with documentation, explaining what was going to happen to my body now that it thought I have a baby to feed.

It was just another reminder of the baby I was not taking home with me, and it depressed me further.

Although I could walk, I was delivered to the exit in a wheelchair, and loaded into my mom's car. We drove home in silence.

I knew this was the best thing for my baby, I knew it was the right thing to do; but I wanted to cry, I wanted to sob. But I held back the tears; I may have given up my baby, but my mom had just said goodbye to her first grandchild. She was experiencing a loss of her own, and there was no reason for me to upset her further—especially while she was driving.

Once home, I plopped down on my little mattress on the floor and listened to music on my stereo.

I put on my new Heart album. I had just purchased it from a small record shop in town earlier that week and hadn't even had time to memorize the lyrics yet—something I did with every album I had. The thought crossed my mind that I should give that much attention to my studies, but music spoke to me—not accounting word problems.

My mom brought me something to eat; and I thought, maybe tomorrow, I'll study for my Tuesday night class. But when Monday came, I felt just as lost. My mom had gone to work; I knew I should study, but I couldn't stop thinking about my baby girl, wondering if she was still in the hospital, or if she had been taken home by her new parents already. All I could do was pray. And so, I did. I prayed that everything would work out as I'd been told it would, I prayed that all of this was part of God's plan.

When I returned to class, no one seemed to notice I'd had my baby; they probably did, but no one said anything. I tried my best to get into a normal routine, to start thinking about my future. My mom suggested I move into the dorm the following quarter at Whitworth College and attend college full time, and the prospect of going to school full time perked me up a little—at least it was a plan. The opportunity to spend more time with Anne and her friends was also appealing. I wasn't sure what I was going to major in, but I was certain this was a step I needed to take. The thought of moving back to Florida didn't seem to make sense anymore.

Ruth had decided to go away to college in Ohio, and June and Paul were planning on moving in together. If I went back to Fort Lauderdale now, I would have no one to stay with; even my sister had moved in with her latest boyfriend.

And it wasn't as though I could work—or even look for a job—without a car.

The fact that it had been eight months since I'd driven a car was a secondary concern. After all I had experienced, coupled with the fact that the cost of living was far more in Florida than it was in Mississippi, there were few reasons for me to return to Florida right away.

I applied for admission to Whitworth and financial aid, while my mom planned her move back to Northern Mississippi. I had always been good in math and was currently taking an Accounting night class, so I thought I'd pursue a degree in Business and Accounting. Living in the dorm was a step toward living on my own, as an adult, without the immediate need to fully support myself, financially.

During my first official visit to the campus as a prospective student, I found out that I would have a dorm room all to myself, since there were only about a dozen females living in the dorm.

The college grounds were so beautiful, with big trees, grassy lawns and historical buildings with extraordinary architecture; founded in 1858, I felt as though I had traveled back in time. Our dorm had hard wood floors and stairs, with large wooden bannisters; and the second floor was replete with a large balcony, overlooking the campus grounds. I soon acquired an interest in the history of the school and the architecture of the historical buildings.

In the midst of preparing for my new college life, something quite strange occurred. While my mom and I were in Jackson for my follow up doctor appointment, we went shopping in a department store for a new set of sheets for my recently acquired double mattress. One of the sales girls approached us, to assist us, I thought. "Excuse me, you look really familiar. Are you the girl who was driving the Mustang that crashed into a tree on the Natchez Trace, last Palm Sunday?"

I was shocked—not only because she recognized me from the accident; but her question made me realize just how much had happened to me during the last eight months. "Yes, I'm the girl." I said.

My mom then explained to her that I was still recovering from the accident—and of course left out the whole part of the recovery whereby I was pregnant and gave birth to a baby.

We also told her that I had enrolled at Whitworth College and would be living in one of the dorms, attending school full time; and we were shopping for things for my room. I just stood there, mostly listening to the conversation between my mom and this salesgirl; when the salesgirl revealed that she had been a passenger in the car I had passed on The Trace, and they had been the ones who stopped to help us. Her father was the one who had performed CPR and brought me *back to life*. She and some of the other family members had driven to the nearest town to get an ambulance sent to the crash site.

She told me that her family had prayed for me quite often after that day and always wondered what had happened to me.

I stood there, listening to her version of events and was completely awestruck that I was meeting a person who had not only witnessed the accident, but whose family had saved my life.

She explained to us that her family was out for a casual Sunday drive and was going under the speed limit, down The Trace, when I passed them. The roads were slick from a little rain that had fallen earlier; and when my front tire hit a pothole on the side of the road, I lost control of the car. She told me that her entire family witnessed the car slam into a tree and immediately pulled over and started helping us.

Her father had just completed an EMT course; and when he realized I had stopped breathing, he performed CPR on me.

I was so amazed that I was running into this girl now—what perfect timing—I wondered if this was God's way of letting her family know that everything had turned out all right for me; and it was an answered prayer for them. It was also a way to satisfy my curiosity, regarding what exactly had happened, from an eye witness.

I thanked her and asked her to thank her family as well. She thanked us for sharing with her and later for our purchase and told me she wished the best for me in college.

After everything I had been through, running into this girl cheered me. I had so many more questions answered that no one could ever confirm. It was a stark reminder of how lucky I was to be alive at all, and now, being given the opportunity to go to college and begin living as an adult, on my own.

My plan was to move into the dorm at the end of November, after the Thanksgiving holiday. But before I officially started college, I decided to travel to Ohio for a week and visit my dad—and this time, Ruth also.

It was so nice to see all of my relatives from my dad's side of the family again. My aunts were all strong women and very independent—as was my dad's girlfriend, who he had met through his sisters shortly after my parent's divorce.

At times, these women could be quite intimidating, but one afternoon my dad's girlfriend and my aunts took me bowling; and we had a wonderful time. I probably wasn't physically healed enough to do so, but I didn't want to discuss my condition with my aunts because I didn't know if my dad had told them about my pregnancy or not. I assumed his girlfriend knew, but I didn't ask her.

I also was able to visit Ruth and spent a couple of days, hanging out with her on the Ohio State University campus. She took me to an end of semester party; and it felt like it had been forever since I had been to a party, with music and people my own age.

Ruth was on her way home to Fort Lauderdale for the school's Holiday break, and I was returning to my new home to prepare for my own college experience.

When I returned to Mississippi, my mom and I officially moved out of our apartment; and I moved into the dorm. Decorating my dorm room made me feel like I was an independent adult. Although I would be sharing a small kitchen and bathroom with the other girls on the floor, I felt like I was truly on my own for the first time in my life.

My simple furnishings consisted of a double mattress and box springs on the floor. I put my small end table next to the bed on one side, with a lamp and an alarm clock upon it and my stereo on the other side. I also had a small dresser, and I hung a long mirror on the wall next to it.

There was only one thing left to do…

I grabbed a roll of heavy tape we had purchased, since the interior walls were made of an old hard plaster; and I went to work. I stood back and looked at my handy work.

It was the perfect beginning to my college experience—a wall covered with posters of Peter Frampton—including the poster from my ICU!

Chapter 9

Culture shock

This was my new life; I was a full-time student at Whitworth College—employed fifteen hours a week through a work study program that included cleaning the dorm, typing and copying papers for some of the professors, and helping fellow students file their financial aid paperwork. Once a week, I also helped out in the kitchen, but that was considered volunteer work.

My mom was working for the Academy in Northern Mississippi and really didn't have the wherewithal to help me financially. But between financial aid and some help from my dad, I was making ends meet. While weekly lunches were included as part of living in the dorm, a handful of us went to the movies or out for pizza quite often, so I had little money left over to buy new clothing or much of anything else. I'd been working hard on getting back into my little black bikini, hoping that a trip to the beach was somewhere in my near future.

I accepted the fact that giving birth to a baby made changes to a woman's body that became permanent; I doubted I'd ever be a size five again.

During the Christmas break, I returned to the Academy to stay at my mom's place. My brother was now attending the Academy, and we all spent Christmas together.

Anne and I returned to Whitworth College for the Spring Quarter and during spring break, we drove down to the coast for a short visit on the beach and then headed up to the Academy for the rest of the week. At the end of the school year, I returned to the Academy to live with my mom for the summer. Edward had been living with my mom in her apartment—which was a converted building on campus—with three bedrooms and two bathrooms, but he flew back to Ohio to visit our Dad during the summer. I wanted so badly to go to Florida, but I was still not driving; and I didn't have a car or any money for gas!

My luck changed when I had the good fortune of traveling to Orlando mid-summer with a family I knew from the Academy. My friend Joe, who had come to see me in the hospital, drove up from Fort Lauderdale and joined us at Disney World. I returned with him to Fort Lauderdale, and he dropped me off at Ruth's house. I was able to stay with her for a couple of weeks; we went to the beach, and I visited old friends. Mostly, I hung out with Ruth and her new boyfriend, since neither one of us drove. I spent a little time with a couple of boys I knew from FLCA who I hadn't seen since I was a sophomore in high school.

One of them invited me to go on a date to a Surf-Expo, and I had an awesome time; but being out on a date was still a new experience for me.

June and Paul were now married and had a baby. It was strange to see June as a mother; I still felt like a child myself and couldn't imagine the responsibilities she had.

I arranged a visit with her; and she confessed her hurt feelings over my decision to keep my pregnancy a secret from her, which implied I didn't trust she could keep it to herself. She had later found out about it from Paul, when William told him about the adoption. I apologized and explained my concerns about William finding out at that time, especially since we were no longer dating.

I didn't see Paul or William during that trip—I felt like it was too soon to contact William; he had not kept in touch with me after the adoption papers were signed.

While I was away in Florida, Anne decided to switch schools and made plans to live at the Academy with her parents and go to Mississippi State University. It was no secret that if you weren't planning to attend Seminary, the degree opportunities at Whitworth College were limited.

I wondered what school would be like without her there.

I was tempted to just stay in Florida, but I really had nowhere to live.

Ruth was headed back to Ohio to finish her Nursing degree, and June and Paul were living in her Grandmother's house now as a family.

Leigh was living with her boyfriend somewhere in Fort Lauderdale, and I hung out with her one day. We had lost touch after I moved to Mississippi with our mom and decided to have my baby. She wanted to show me the journal she had kept while I was in the hospital. I cried as I read her daily entries about visiting me in the ICU and how my family tried to get me to respond to them, but how I showed no signs of life. It was so touching—I hadn't realized how serious my condition was when I was in my coma.

The first thing I did on my return to Mississippi was to sign up for a driver's education course so I could learn to drive again.

I'll never forget the day the instructor took us out on the Natchez Trace Parkway. It had been more than a year since I'd driven a car, but since I was the only one in the class with a driver's license, and he was trying to teach us all defensive driving; it was easier to instruct the other students while I was driving the van. With Anne transferring schools; I would be stuck in Brookhaven, always trying to find rides, if I didn't start driving again. My goal was to buy a car as soon as possible, although I had no idea how I was going to accomplish that.

Even though Anne was gone, I had decided to return to Whitworth College. The new year brought in a new group of students, including a couple of nice looking young men. Some of the students I knew from our former church in Fort Lauderdale. Some former students were returning and familiar faces were coming in, so it still felt comfortable at school to me. I wasn't really focusing on a major, so I continued taking business and Bible courses.

Anne and Dan were now engaged, and I often hitched rides back to the Academy with Dan. He was now living in Baton Rouge and returned to the Academy in Northern Mississippi a couple of weekends a month, so he would pick me up on his way through Brookhaven. During our visit over the Christmas holiday, my mom asked me if I wanted to buy her car. She had been living and working at the Academy for over a year now, along with my Aunt and Uncle, and found she was typically traveling most places with one of them. Since my mom had borrowed money from my insurance settlement, she offered to give me the car instead of repaying the remainder of the money she still owed me. I really didn't want to drive around in a Chevy Impala, but it was available; and the financing terms, so to speak, were agreeable.

Having my own car gave me a greater sense of independence and made me feel even more like I was an adult and on my own.

Of course, the car was also big enough that I could carry around a large group of friends; and since it only got about ten miles to the gallon, the fact that everyone pitched in for gas helped greatly.

One wise old Professor at Whitworth had convinced me at the beginning of my second school year that if I worked a little bit harder and studied this year, I could make all A's in my classes. I decided to take his advice, and I had a straight A report card that first Quarter. While hesitant, I went out with a couple of the new boys at school; although, most of the time, these outings were usually in a group setting. I also tutored a couple of the boys in English; and they, in turn, took me out to eat as repayment. I continued to make straight A's in all of my classes; and at one point, I considered becoming a teacher.

But my real love was Fashion Design—which meant I couldn't finish my education at Whitworth College. So, I was considering transferring to another college after the end of the school year—maybe in Mississippi, maybe in Florida.

Since Edward was attending high school now at the Academy, I often drove there to watch him play football and basketball. I made a habit of stopping in at the restaurant/bar at the TGI Friday's in Jackson on my way home on Fridays and became friends with a couple of the bartenders.

The drinking age in Mississippi was twenty-one; but when I lived in Florida, it had been eighteen. I had been able to drink legally in Florida since I was eighteen, and it seemed stupid that I wasn't allowed to do so in Mississippi. Since I wasn't old enough to drink in Mississippi, one of my college friends gave me her old identification card; and I used it the first few times I went there. Her middle name was the same as my first name, so it worked.

But things didn't always work out in my favor. I decided to stop into the TGI Friday's on my way to a *Heart* concert in Jackson, in April 1980. I was so excited to go see Ann and Nancy Wilson and their band live again. I'd taken some old clothes I had from high school and something I found at a second hand store and recycled them into an awesome outfit I'd made just for the concert. I was wearing black satin pants and a matching strapless shirt, with a black and copper herringbone smoking jacket—and five inch heeled sandals. Although I thought I looked especially grown up, sipping my beer at the bar, a man from behind it approached me and asked for proof of my age; but I had long since returned my friend's identification card. I explained I didn't have my ID card with me, all of the bartenders knew me there; so I didn't think it would be an issue. Instead, he took my drink and said sternly, "No ID, no alcohol!"

I found out later he was from the liquor board. But at the time, I determined I wasn't going to let him ruin my night.

Having been *kicked out* of the bar, I left quickly; and I ended up at the concert venue far too early. The parking lot was close to empty; but I sat there, trying to pass the time. Eventually, I needed to use the restroom. I got out of my car and wandered around the building, trying to find a way in. I found a door on the far side of the building unlocked, and walked right in. I noticed the only people in the hallways were T-shirt vendors, decked out in rock-and-roll outfits. I soon realized that because of my outfit, they must have thought I was one of them; and so no one seemed to take notice of my presence. I walked into the restroom and while I was in the stall, I heard someone come into the restroom. I looked out through the crack of the stall door and saw a female security guard, so I stayed in the stall until she left and then went back out into the hallway. I was going to return to my car but noticed some double-doors that were partially open, clearly leading into the arena. I stepped up to the doorway and peeked through—to my surprise, I saw Ann and Nancy Wilson, along with their band, on stage and dressed in jeans, singing "When a Man Loves a Woman," a cappella. It was an awesome sight to see—and hear.

Then a loud male voice came from somewhere inside the arena, "Hey, you, you're not allowed in here!"

I just shut the door, hurried back to the restroom, and hid in the stall again.

Soon after, a couple of other girls came into the restroom. I asked them if they were vendors; they said they were not, but had just walked into an unlocked side door and come in to use the restroom. I told them I'd done the same thing. They asked if I had a ticket; I told them I did. None of us had shown our tickets to anyone, and we were all wondering if there was a way to resell our tickets outside. We decided to wait until after the doors *officially* opened, and we would see if we could figure out something when other people started coming in.

Having *snuck in* through the back/side door, we were the first people to enter the arena when the doors officially opened and were able to stand right at the edge of the stage. One of the girls found her brother, and she persuaded him to go back outside and sell our tickets. I told him if he got me a Heart T-shirt, he could keep the rest of the money from selling my ticket. I had no idea who these people were, but obviously, I was very trusting. To my pleasure, he returned a short time later and handed me the T-shirt.

I ended up standing right up front, and I could actually talk to Ann and Nancy when they came on stage. I was especially tall in my five-inch heels; and dressed the way I was, with my long, blonde hair, I must have stood out.

Not only did they notice me, Nancy actually commented on how great my *smoking jacket* was.

They weren't the only ones who noticed me. A young man named Jeff, who had actually gone to school with Edward, was standing on the floor in the crowd about half-way back from the stage. His friend, Thomas, had made a comment about the blonde up front and Jeff realized who I was. He explained our connection, but Thomas didn't believe him. Jeff insisted he knew me, and the two of them made their way up to the front; and Jeff introduced me to Thomas. With my heels on, he was shorter than me; but he was a good-looking guy, with reddish-brown, shoulder length wavy hair and an awesome smile. The two of them stayed up front with us for the rest of the show.

After the concert was over, my new girlfriends left, and so did Jeff. Thomas and I stayed in the hallway, talking and getting to know each other. When two members of Heart, Roger Fisher and Mike Derosier, came out of a side door and into the hallway to take pictures with fans; Thomas asked me if I wanted go over there to have my picture taken with them. "No, I'm talking to you right now," I replied.

As the place cleared out, Thomas asked me if I could give him a ride to his sister's apartment. I told him, "Yes". I was on my own, and had no one checking up on me. Perhaps I was being too trusting again, but he was Jeff's friend, and I wasn't too concerned.

We left in my car and drove to a nearby park, so we could continue talking. Thomas told me he played guitar in a band, and we talked about music and exchanged stories of concerts we had been to, as we listened to the radio for hours. I was surprised my car battery didn't die.

Billy Joel's new hit played on the radio more than once that night, and "You May Be Right" (I may be crazy) became our song.

We drove to Thomas' sister's garage apartment, and all the lights were off—it was so late that he didn't want to wake them. We stayed up talking most of the night and ended up sleeping in my car outside of his sister's apartment. Luckily it was April, so it wasn't too cold at night. When daylight came, I wondered if anyone at Whitworth College might be worried about my absence; and I told Thomas I needed to leave. I also told him to make sure he told his friend, Jeff, that nothing had happened between us; or I would be in serious trouble if/when my brother found out that I left the concert with his friend.

Thomas wrote his phone number on a brown paper bag with a lime green crayon he found in the garage, and I told him I would call him as soon as I was able. I hurried back to school, having to wake somebody up to let me back into the dorm. I made up a story about not wanting to drive home after the concert, so I had stayed the night with a friend.

Technically, it was the truth.

I called Thomas as soon as I could, and we exchanged addresses so we could write to each other. We wrote every week for the last four weeks of the school year. But when I told him I was going to Fort Lauderdale for the summer, he thought he'd never hear from me again. I gave him Ruth's address in Fort Lauderdale, where I would be staying, and told him I would write to him as soon as I got to Florida.

Chapter 10

Change of plans

1980

Ruth was still away at school when I arrived in Florida this time, but her mom let me stay in her room. She also made a deal with me; if I contributed toward the utility bills, I could stay the entire summer, and I eagerly agreed.

I was so happy to have a car this time around. I no longer had to depend on anyone else for rides. I was also able to drive myself to church and watch June play piano for the church choir. It was difficult to find a lot of time to spend with June, besides at church, now that she had a husband and a child. I also reconnected with several of my other church friends.

When Ruth got home, we spent most of our time at the beach, lying in the sun and walking up and down the strip, and it felt like old times. We went out to our favorite hang outs at night with friends—and even went to Key West one weekend. I also continued writing to Thomas over the summer.

Before I had left Mississippi for my summer in Fort Lauderdale, I had decided, with encouragement from Anne, to transfer from Whitworth College to Mississippi State University.

It was time for me to choose a college major.

In discussing my college credits to date, coupled with my personal interests, my college guidance counselor and I determined Fashion Merchandising was where I should focus my studies. I wasn't sure how this degree would transfer out into the real world, since I had an interest in fashion design and this would actually take me closer to becoming a buyer, but I still had a couple of years to figure out the details.

When I shared my plans with Thomas, he had seemed disappointed. "You should have transferred to Southern," he said. "It's more artsy, and besides, I was planning on trying to go there." This surprised me. It was too late for me to change my mind, but his comments revealed he hoped to see more of me. As far as I was concerned, we were more friends and pen pals than anything else.

At the end of the summer, I returned to Mississippi; I packed up my wardrobe, said goodbye to my mom, and took off for Mississippi State University. Anne and I would be roommates in one of the dorms on campus.

Anne and I became friends with some other girls in our dorm and were invited to become *Little Sisters* in a Fraternity. While we weren't Fraternity members, per se, we were assigned to help plan parties and help with *Rush* weeks.

This was when they invited all the new male students to visit the Fraternity to see if they wanted to pledge the fraternity and become members. Being *Little Sisters* allowed us to be involved in most of the Fraternity events, and we had a lot of fun planning parties and fundraisers and attending them. I also enjoyed designing and making costumes for the themed parties.

My course plan gave me additional opportunities to design and sew clothing. But even though I enjoyed most of my classes, I was doing more partying than studying, and my grades were suffering.

When the year ended, we decided to move out of the dorm on campus.

The college was located in a city called Starkville, and Anne had made plans to work in town that summer while taking extra classes, so the next school year she would have a lighter class load and could live at home to save money and drive back and forth to school a couple of days a week. Since I was loosing Anne as a dorm mate, I had planned on moving into a two bedroom duplex with a couple of the girls I'd met at school. The duplex was within walking distance of the Frat house. I asked Anne to take my place in the duplex for the summer, so I could return to Fort Lauderdale one last time before I graduated.

Terrie, a friend I'd known from high school and church, was attending college in Jackson; and she rode with me to Fort Lauderdale and invited me to stay with her family the first week I arrived.

I'd been writing to church friends, inquiring about available summer jobs and rooms for rent. I found a woman who agreed to rent a room to me in her house, complete with a kitchenette, a bathroom, and a private entrance. I took on two part time jobs; one at a department store, named Burdine's, and the other at Pizza Hut. Anne was currently working at one of the Pizza Huts in Starkville; and I hoped my stint in Fort Lauderdale would help me get hired there in the fall, after she moved home. I felt as though I was entirely on my own again, but this time, in Fort Lauderdale.

My schedule allowed me to go the beach almost every morning, except for the 2 or 3 mornings I worked construction with an old friend of mine; and I tried to catch the sunrise as often as I could. I spent what free time I had with June and Ruth or old friends I knew from high school or church.

Leigh had moved into her finance's house in Jupiter; and so when I could get a couple of days off in a row from both of my jobs, I would drive up to visit them. I remember being at Leigh's and Kyle's house, and they were making margaritas for us while we hung out by their pool.

Kyle, a concert promoter and car collector, handed me a pair of drumsticks. "They're from the Peter Frampton concert, back in 1976. Your sister told me you all went to the show together, and you're a big fan. Peter gave these to me as a souvenir. I want to give them to you." That was such a cool gift to give me—and I still have them!

The next time I went to visit them, I brought Kyle a Godiva chocolate Mercedes from the store where I worked—although it was a Coupe by the time I arrived (having no A/C in my Impala)!

I hadn't seen William in three years, and it wasn't an easy thing to do; but I also decided to get in touch with him. I wasn't sure how this meeting would go, but I was told by a friend that he had just returned from visiting relatives abroad; and he wanted to see me. I went to his house, reflecting on the many parties I had attended there with my friends. We sat at the dining room table, drinking wine, eating cheese and crackers, and talking about our lives since we had last seen each other. He seemed to be doing well; although he and George were both still living at home with their mom, they were each running their own businesses. William asked me about the pregnancy, the adoption, where I lived in Mississippi, and if I was ever coming back to Florida. I told him a little about the pregnancy and how difficult it had been to be a single, pregnant teen in Mississippi.

I told him a little about the adoption and also a little bit about the adoptive parents.

I got the impression that he wasn't really interested in the details, but I told him I had no way of knowing where our daughter was or how to find her; but I felt comfortable that her new parents were a good, stable, Christian couple. I admitted I wasn't sure if I would ever move back to Fort Lauderdale permanently, but that my immediate plan was to stay in college and finish my degree. After three years of College, I wanted to graduate with some sort of a degree that would help me land a good career in the future.

It turned out that William's family did find out about our baby, because his mom found the letter I had sent to him. It also turned out that his grandmother was a lawyer and represented him on his side of the adoption. I had no idea his family knew anything about our baby and the adoption —this really surprised me. It also put some doubts in mind about how involved they were in the adoption.

I'm not sure where William's mom was that night, but I was glad she was away—I'm not sure she would have liked to have seen me in her house—after what William and I had been through. But when George walked through the living room, and I said hello to him; I could tell I was the last person he expected to see there.

William and I talked for hours, and I found a new level of comfort with him. I suppose the things that had happened between us had bound us somehow, made us feel connected, like family.

But, that would be the last time I saw William for twenty years.

Chapter 11

Fourth year and summer school

1981

It was my fourth year of college. Classes, studying, work, and parties; that was my schedule. The job at the Pizza Hut in Starkville didn't exactly pan out how I had hoped, so I earned money again through work study jobs on campus.

In October, Anne and I and a couple of our girlfriends from the Fraternity drove to Jackson for a weekend Fraternity Homecoming party. The party started on Friday night and was to last until Sunday afternoon, but since we weren't going to the game; we only planned on spending all of Saturday in town. When we arrived in Jackson, we went shopping and out to lunch. When we got to the party though, I realized how close we were to where Thomas lived. I called him and invited him to come to the party too.

The rest of the girls were planning to return to campus that night, but Thomas and I wanted to go out; so I made arrangements to spend the night at a girlfriend's house and get a ride back to campus the next day.

Thomas had borrowed his younger sister's car, so we went to a dance club where the bar supplied the mixers, and the club-goers supplied the liquor. It was something I had never seen in Florida; but on the other hand, Mississippi was still foreign to me.

It wasn't all that exciting of a club, but they played great music; the new Foreigner song, *Waiting for a Girl Like You*, was the last one we heard.

Thomas invited me to go over to his older sister's place, the same garage apartment where I had dropped him off the night we met, where we could hang out and talk. She and her boyfriend were in the process of moving out, but they still had most of their furniture there. It turned out that his sister and her boyfriend were staying at his mom's house that night, but Thomas knew where the spare key was hidden.

The electricity had been turned off, so it was a little cold in the apartment, but Thomas found some blankets and candles. We talked most of the night, and ended up falling asleep in the apartment. When we finally awoke and drove to my friend's house, it was 4 am. Thomas needed to get his sister's car back to her, so she could go to work that morning.

Thomas kissed me goodbye and told me he loved me. But he also told me that I was too good for him...

The rest of the day was one disaster after another—everyone was asleep at my friend's house when I arrived, and I had to wake somebody up to get in. I was shown to an empty room where I could sleep until everyone else was awake. Once everyone woke up; I discovered even with all the cars heading back to campus, not one of them had room for me. I had brought nothing with me, not even a toothbrush; and now I was without a way back to campus. I felt like such an imposition. I wished more than ever I would have driven my own car to Jackson, but I couldn't afford the extra gas money.

My friends called some other friends and found one of the *little sisters* I knew who said I could ride back to campus with her and her boyfriend. I got a ride to the girl's house but arrived to discover she was on her way to church with her boyfriend and her mother, not ready to drive back to the college yet. I spent the rest of the morning, sitting in their family room with her dad, feeling entirely uncomfortable, stuck in the jeans and sweater I was now wearing for the second day. But with all of that, none of it really mattered to me—because Thomas had told me he loved me.

I spent the ride back to campus curled up in the backseat of my friend's Volkswagen bug, with she and her boyfriend in the front seats, replaying the events of the night before over and over in my mind.

Long distance calls were still too expensive, so Thomas and I maintained our relationship primarily through letters. Money was so tight in fact, that by the end of the semester, I had to move out of the duplex and back to the Academy, carpooling back and forth to campus with Anne two days per week.

In the spring, I got a job at a new restaurant/bar that was just opening near campus. They were going to feature live music on the weekends in the bar, but they were still in the process of building the restaurant. The bar was located in a hotel; and I would be working as a cocktail waitress, biding my time for the restaurant to open. Now that I had a job near the college, I asked my former roommates if I could move back in for the last few months of the semester. I told them if need be, I would sleep on a beach lounge chair in the large, walk-in closet in the living room. They agreed, but it was not the best of situations. The closet had spiders, and I ended up sleeping on a beach lounge chair in the living room most of the time.

I'd never worked as a cocktail waitress but caught on pretty quickly. The clientele was mixed—business men, hotel guests, and college students. Obviously, the business men tipped much better than the college students. Happy hour was crazy; it started in the late afternoons or before the live music on weekends and featured three-for-one drink specials—with the drinks served in mason jars.

If a table of four sat down, I would end up carrying twelve mason jars full of alcohol to the table, across the room, all for the price of four drinks. But the tips rolled in, and I was making nearly a hundred dollars a night, more than I'd made at any other job in Starkville.

By the time summer came, the restaurant still hadn't opened. I had planned on going to summer school, but we had to move out of our duplex near campus; and the dorms were closed until summer school started. I took a few days off from the bar and took my mom to Pensacola over the holiday weekend, where she would be catching a bus to Merritt Island to spend the summer working with a teen mission. Before my mom left for her trip, the two of us spent a few days in Pensacola together on the beach and camping at the State park for a couple of nights—which really meant my mom sleeping on a beach lounge chair and me, sleeping in the back seat of my car.

Wandering around Pensacola, wearing clothing I had designed and sewn myself, gave me an idea…after graduation, I could design beachwear for a living and make my home on the coast. The thought of this gave me great joy—I was now excited to go back and finish my last year of college.

I said goodbye to my mom and put her on the bus.

I had intended on spending one last day on the beach but instead, I went back to the campground, showered, got dressed and packed up my things; so I could start my drive to Jackson. I was going to see Thomas and share with him my future plans.

When I arrived in Jackson and telephoned him, he wasn't home. I had to try several times, and it was becoming embarrassing to have to keep calling. When I finally reached him, he said he didn't have access to a car but was going to ride his bike to meet me. I wondered why he didn't ask me to come and get him, and the thought crossed my mind that maybe he didn't want me to see where he lived. I had never seen his house or met his parents and we had been friends for over two years now.

Thomas finally showed up to the TGI Fridays where we had met before, not surprisingly, a little on the sweaty side.

I knew Thomas had always liked to draw and was hoping to use his talent to get a job someday, so we talked during lunch about my discovery while in Pensacola. I told him that when I graduated, I wanted to move to the coast and design and make beachwear; and I hoped he could use his talent to airbrush designs on my clothing. I also told him I had a birthday gift for him, which seemed to surprise him.

I gave him a shirt I had purchased in Pensacola; it was a medical scrub shirt and had an airbrushed beach design on the pocket. I suggested to him that we could sell similar items.

He told me it was so sweet of me to get him a birthday present, but he still thought I was too good for him. This was the second time he'd told me this, and it was really starting to confuse me. I just didn't understand why he thought this—he saw something in me that I didn't see.

Before I left that afternoon, Thomas ended up telling me that he was dating someone new, and we probably shouldn't see each other anymore. He said he had always wanted us to be more than friends, but he knew that would never happen; because we were so different. I told him I hoped we could still be friends and pen pals, but I understood if he didn't see a future with me. I was hurt, but I felt that he wasn't really rejecting me; he was trying to show me how different our lifestyles were, and why we wouldn't work as a couple.

After seeing Thomas, I drove back to the Academy. The ninety minute drive up the Trace gave me a chance to really think about my future. I stayed at my mom's place for a few days, by myself, while I washed and repacked the clothes I wanted to take back to school for the summer semesters.

Even though I had told the bar that I wanted to come back to work at the restaurant when I returned to Starkville, I found the restaurant had still not opened. The bar was too slow for them to hire me back, as most of the college students had left town for the summer. I returned, once again, to work study positions on campus to make a little money. I ended up working in the library a little during the days and at the campus radio station on Wednesday nights.

The jobs were fun, but once again, I was living on granola bars and yogurt and barely able to pay for books or gas for my car to get anywhere. I couldn't return home all summer; but there really was no reason to go back to the Academy, with my mom out of the country on a mission trip.

I was now living in a dorm on campus that was paid for through financial aid and student loans. I had a roommate, named Sally; and she seemed nice, so we started spending time together. A couple of weeks into the semester, she told me she knew a guy who lived in Starkville that she wanted me to meet. His name was Ethan.

Ethan wasn't a college student, so I'm not sure how they knew each other; but one night we all went out and she introduced the two of us. We hit it off, and it was nice to have someone else pay for our drinks that night.

Ethan seemed very kind and started taking me out to eat and to clubs to listen to music and go dancing, even though this didn't seem like his kind of thing. I wasn't sure if I was starting to have real feelings for Ethan or if I just liked the fact that someone was interested in me and taking me out—and feeding me. We didn't really have a lot in common. He wasn't the kind of person to hang out on a beach, which was not surprising with his red hair and pale skin; and he was mostly into country music, which did not really appeal to me much. But he was nice to spend time with, and so we dated for the rest of the summer.

I didn't do very well in my classes though—there was just too much work to do and not enough time to study with the accelerated summer schedule and working and going out—but I did pass all of them, and that's really what mattered—to me!

At the end of the summer, I went home to the Academy for a week because the dorm had closed, and I had nowhere else to live until I could move back into the dorm for the fall semester. Besides, my mom was back now from her summer mission trip. (I believe she took a bus home this time from Florida and my Aunt Lora picked her up from the bus station.)

I had been unable to drive anywhere much because I still had no money to put gas in my *boat of a car.*

When I returned to the dorm on campus for my last two semesters of college, my new dorm mate turned out to be from New Orleans. She was really cool, petite and adorable; and so I took her with me to the Frat house, so she could become a *Little Sister* and help with parties and *Rush* weeks too. I thought everyone really liked her, but the head of the Fraternity, someone new who I really didn't know, determined she dressed to *scantily* and told me that she would have to change her clothing if she wanted to hang out at the Frat house.

The two of us decided neither of us would be volunteering our time to help them anymore. I was spending a lot of time with Ethan anyway and didn't really have much free time.

Ethan and I had even been talking about future plans. He told me he didn't want to stay in Starkville, but he wanted to move to a larger city to find a better job. This was something I had planned on doing as soon as I graduated.

Ethan was an aluminum welder and was good at his job, so he figured he could work a lot of other places. I still wanted to move to the coast—Pensacola, Panama City or maybe Destin—to start my beachwear store. Now it seemed Ethan might be interested in moving wherever I wanted to go, and so I was starting to picture a future with him.

I had planned on moving to Jackson mid semester for my internship, to work part time as a costume designer in the local theatre. But at the last minute, the theatre that had offered me the position called my counselor, and said they couldn't afford to pay me. While some friends of ours had offered me a free place to live, I would still need food and gas money; so my plans had to change.

I ended up having to take a last minute job in the crystal, silver and china department at a large retail store. This was not what I wanted to do with my Fashion Merchandising degree, especially after all the summers I had spent working at Burdine's; but at this point, I had no other option.

Before I left campus, the dorm was requiring me to put a deposit on my room for the following semester, but I had no *extra* money and had to give up my room—which also meant I had to say goodbye to my awesome roommate.

My mom had since moved into her own, larger apartment at the Academy; and with Edward living away at college, she now had a spare room available for me where she was storing my furniture. I packed all of my personal things and moved them back to the Academy, awaiting my new temporary position in Jackson.

Chapter 12

Defiant youth

1982

I was living with my mom for a short time, preparing to move to Jackson, when one night she came into my room and woke me up. She sat on my bed and began to question why I was never in my dorm room when my family called me at school and why my roommate always told everyone I must be in the restroom or in the library, studying.

I couldn't believe she would wake me up and ask me these things now. And then she wanted to know if I had been carrying on a relationship with a *boy*—behind her back!

I was twenty-two years old and had been living, mostly on my own, since I was eighteen. I could not believe she was questioning me about my personal life like I was a child. Did I have to have my mother's permission to date someone? She told me that if I was going to carry on a relationship without her knowledge and consent, I was not welcomed to live under her roof. Even though, technically, my furniture had spent more time *living* in her apartment than I ever had.

I realize now that she was just concerned for my well being, but her approach put me on the defensive.

We had never really discussed boys or dating when I was growing up; and until I found out I was pregnant, we had never discussed sex. Now, as an adult, older than she was when she had married my dad and given birth to my older sister; she wanted to know who I was seeing and what I was doing. I was half asleep and not about to sit up in bed and tell her all about my life during the last several months, while she was away on a mission trip; and I was trying to support myself at college.

She had never asked me about my personal life before, and it wasn't going to start now.

Instead, I got out of bed and called Ethan. The next day, he and a friend drove to the Academy; and we packed up all my stuff into his truck, and I moved it into his apartment in Starkville.

I was still planning to move to Jackson temporarily for work, but Ethan told me that my furniture could stay with him while I was away. He had an extra (unfurnished) bedroom and didn't seem to mind. I hadn't known Ethan but for a few months, and I didn't plan on moving in with him permanently, but he told me I could keep my things at his place until I returned and found another place for them. We left the Academy and drove back to Starkville.

I wasn't sure what Ethan was going to tell his parents about the now furnished bedroom he had, since they owned the apartment building he lived in; but I had met them during the summer, and his father, at least, seemed to like me.

I was back in Starkville for less than a week before I packed up my Impala with everything I would need in Jackson and took off for my new temporary home.

The couple I stayed with were the *parents* of the couple I had gone to Orlando with the summer of 1979, and so I had met them before. They were such a kind and generous couple—they gave me my own bedroom and bathroom, washed all my towels and sheets and kept me fed—if I was going to be at home in the evenings.

I stayed in Jackson for about eight weeks, from the middle of October until the middle of December.

It was about a two hour drive each way from Starkville, and I couldn't afford the gas in my Impala to drive back and forth; plus I only had one day at a time off work, which was typical in retail. Ethan's and my work schedules made it difficult to be together, so we talked on the phone often. A few times he drove down to Jackson to see me over the weekend, and we spent the night in a hotel when I had the next day off work.

There was one dilemma about living in Jackson though; now that I was so close to where Thomas lived, we had the opportunity to talk on the phone also, without racking up long distance charges. He had written me a letter the previous year, after our night together and apologized, and said he knew it wasn't right. He said he knew I wasn't *that type of girl,* and he apologized for taking advantage of me and for telling me that he loved me. I wrote back to him and told him it was not his fault, and he did not *take advantage* of me.

We never discussed that night again.

We were both dating other people now and decided it was best not to see each other in person, but we thought we could remain friends and pen pals. I still had feelings for him, but Thomas again made comments that implied he thought he wasn't good enough for me. I felt this was because he saw me as a soon to be college graduate, and he was still unable to afford to go to college; and at the time, he had an unfulfilling job.

All I could think was that he seemed to have his head together better than I did, even if he didn't realize it.

The last time Ethan came to visit me in Jackson, in December—and to my complete surprise—he proposed to me. This was entirely unexpected. By this time, we had only known each other for about six months, but I think he was afraid of losing me.

With all of my belongings in his apartment in Starkville, and me in Jackson; I kind of felt trapped. I accepted the ring he gave me; although, truthfully, I don't even recall if I actually said, "Yes". I'm not sure I was as excited as I should have been either. The ring was white gold, with a quarter-carat diamond solitaire; which, to be honest, was beautiful, but wasn't really my style. We had never even talked about marriage, which meant we had never discussed engagement rings either. I had always worn 14k or 18k yellow gold (which coincidentally, went very well with my blonde hair and a tan). I wasn't being materialistic; I just thought, in the back of my mind, that these are the kinds of things you should know about someone if you are planning on spending the rest of your life with him or her.

But instead of giving in to my doubts, I accepted the ring; and I was now engaged.

Since Ethan had always told me that he disliked his job in West Point, I was excited when he agreed that once I graduated, we could move to the coast. He knew I wanted to work somewhere close to the beach and live out my dream of designing beachwear. But when we began discussing wedding dates in the future, plans to move seemed to be put on hold.

However, we both agreed we should set our wedding date for a year after graduation.

This would give me time to travel on my own, if needed, and find a decent job and decide for sure what I wanted to do with my degree. This would also give us time to get to know each other better before Ethan quit his job and moved away from Mississippi and before we got married and started a family.

During the Christmas holiday, my mom invited Ethan and I over for dinner because she wanted to officially meet him and wanted to try to mend things between us. When Ethan and I told her we were engaged, instead of being happy for us, she only wanted to know how soon we were getting married. We told her we were going to wait at least a year or so after I graduated because we didn't feel we were ready to plan a wedding; with me just graduating from college the following May. I wanted a chance to travel and get a good job, possibly on the coast. She was not at all happy with the idea of us living together and told us so. I wanted to say to her, "Yes, we are living together, but we hadn't planned that, either".

But I didn't.

My mom told me that my dad would really like to walk one of his daughters down the aisle, and hadn't had a chance to do so, being that my sister eloped at the age of seventeen. Although my sister had since remarried, her second wedding had been unconventional, and so the *walking a daughter down the aisle* was going to fall on my shoulders.

I said I would be happy to have my father walk me down the aisle—in a year or so, when we planned to marry. But my mother replied that due to my father's health condition, he might not live another year. She said when my father had told Edward and me about his cancer the previous year, he hadn't really revealed to us how bad it was because he didn't want us to worry. My Dad and I had never been very close, so I didn't discuss too many personal things with him.

I was going to be the first in my family to graduate from college, and my dad was planning on traveling to Mississippi for my graduation. "Wouldn't it be nice," she said, "if you could arrange your wedding for the same weekend as your graduation so that you wouldn't have to be concerned about your father not being able to attend it at a later date?"

I couldn't believe it! I was twenty-two years old, and my mother was still telling me what to do. While I understood her concern about my dad's health, I also felt as though she were manipulating the entire situation due to her dissatisfaction over our living arrangement.

But her methods paid off.

After that conversation, I got caught up in the whirlwind of being engaged and trying to plan a wedding.

I was also trying to graduate from college, deciding where I wanted to start my career, and wondering where we were going to live.

It seemed most of my previous dreams were beginning to disappear though.

Our families thought Ethan and I were compatible. We attended pre marital classes with my Uncle Harold, and even he thought we both wanted the same things in life. He thought we both believed in God and wanted to please Him and my family by getting married and not just living together.

It didn't seem to matter that Ethan and I still hadn't discussed our plans for after I graduated. Nor had we discussed what either of us thought about having children; although I had revealed to Ethan early on in our relationship that I had given up a baby girl for adoption when I was eighteen.

But now, I had a wedding to plan and that was taking up all my free time.

When I lived on campus, I had walked past the campus chapel on a daily basis and had always thought that it would be an awesome place to hold an outdoor wedding, and many students had held their weddings there.

Unfortunately, I wasn't the only one who thought it was a great idea, and the chapel was unavailable to us the entire weekend of my graduation, nor the weekend before or after my graduation. This just added to my stress and made me feel even less in control of my destiny.

Why do I have to do this now? I have enough to do just trying to pass all of my classes and graduate!

I went to talk to the President of the school of Agriculture & Home Economics, as all the students in the college do before they graduate. I explained to him why I was practically failing my statistics class; "I don't understand the teacher well enough to learn from him, so I've had to rely solely on the textbook and my notes". "I am also trying to plan a wedding, while my dad, who has cancer, is going to be here from Ohio for my graduation," I explained. "As for the wedding itself, I still can't find a venue I can afford where we can hold the ceremony, that is available graduation weekend."

When I described my dilemma with the chapel, my school's President told me that the University President's campus house—at least the backyard area—would probably be available if I wanted to use it. He told me I should contact the University President and just ask him.

I learned that the University President was given a house to live in while working at the University, but he and his family didn't live there.

The backyard and gazebo of that house were available, so we could have our ceremony there. I also found out that the Baptist Student Union (a building I had actually been to for student church services a couple of times) was available for rent for a small fee—we could use that for the reception.

Knowing I wasn't working and couldn't pay for a wedding, let alone a dress, my Dad gave me $400 to help with the expenses. I made my own wedding dress, along with the peach and white bridesmaid and flower girl dresses. The men would be dressed in khaki and white. I was surprised when I passed all four of my classes my final semester with everything else that was going on.

I didn't really have a best friend in Mississippi who I would ask to be my maid of honor. I guess I could have asked Anne, but since she graduated and started working at the Academy, and I moved permanently to Starkville; we didn't really hang out much anymore. While Ruth and I had continued communicating by writing letters, I'd lost touch with June. But Ruth was busy now working as a nurse in Fort Lauderdale, and June was married with a couple of children. They had never traveled to Mississippi to visit me since I had moved there, and I suppose I thought asking them now would have been inconvenient, so Sally became my maid of honor. She was the one who had introduced me to Ethan, so it only made sense.

The day of my graduation, which happened to fall on Friday the thirteenth, was a little hectic. I had been busy planning our wedding and planned to attend a very large graduation ceremony in the coliseum with my family; which included my mom, my dad, my dad's sister, Edward and Ethan—the night before our wedding. It was a long ceremony, but I will never forget the smiles on my family's faces as I walked passed them to get my diploma. Afterwards, we all went out to eat; and since we were in Mississippi, my out-of-town family wanted to try crawfish. This was something I did not eat, and I ended up waiting an hour for my steak dinner.

Later that evening, Ethan left to stay at his best friend/best man's apartment—as he would be getting ready at Dave's, and I would be getting ready at our apartment. We had decided we would not see each other the day of the wedding until the ceremony.

While I was getting ready, my phone rang—it was Thomas. He said he had just been thinking about me and wanted to congratulate me on graduating.

I had written to him after I left Jackson and told him that Ethan proposed, but we didn't plan on getting married until after I graduated and had a chance to find a good job, possibly on the coast. He had asked me to keep in touch, but I got too busy with everything to write.

I told him I was getting married that very day, and he was a little shocked, to say the least. I explained to him that my family was in town for my graduation, and so *we* had decided to move up our wedding date since my dad was sick. Thomas understood—his father had died unexpectedly a few years earlier. He wished me the best and told me maybe he'd talk to me again—someday. I still had feelings for Thomas, but I didn't know him well enough to say I ever loved him. The timing was never quite right between us; it seemed we were never meant to be more than just friends.

Sally came and picked me up about thirty minutes before the ceremony, although we were not far from campus.

Both Ethan's and my families had made the cakes and other snacks for the reception and delivered them to the student union already. My family had brought all the chairs in the back of a truck from the Academy; and when we parked the car, I could see some of my family and friends still setting them up in the yard and putting the finishing touches on the gazebo for the ceremony. Two other friends of mine, who hadn't known each other before this event, were setting up a keyboard and guitar, to play and sing together during the ceremony. I could also see that some of the guests were arriving.

Sally and I walked to the side of the house, where we would wait with our flower girl and my dad for the ceremony to begin.

When the music started, Ethan and Dave walked over to stand by my Uncle Harold, who was under the small gazebo, ready to perform the ceremony.

We sent my flower girl on her way, but she was too shy to walk alone. Sally joined her and held her hand and the basket of rose petals while she tossed the petals on the walkway. My Dad and I stood there, watching and smiling, though I was terribly nervous inside. I was also feeling very self-conscious about my dress and wondering if it was too low in the back and if my bra was showing. I hadn't thought to try to look in the mirror before I left my apartment or ask my maid of honor to check it out for me. I do remember thinking about it though as I walked down the brick pathway and the wind blew my hair off my back and into my face.

My dad walked me to the front and *gave me away*.

My Uncle Harold performed our ceremony, which was very traditional—no custom vows were written.

I felt like I was in a daze most of the time and even tried to put the wedding band on Ethan's right hand. My Uncle said a prayer at the end of the ceremony and introduced us as "Mr. and Mrs."

We kissed and walked back up the walkway to the end and off into the grass to have photos taken by another friend of Ethan's. During this time, everyone else moved to the student union; and after 30 minutes or so, we joined them.

The photographer smuggled in a small cooler with champagne, and I was surprised when we all had a champagne toast—even my mother, who I'd never seen drink an alcoholic beverage.

Unfortunately, the air conditioner in the student union broke down during the reception, and I remember our wedding cake tilting to one side. But it turned out to be a pretty nice, small wedding; although having had my graduation the night before, was exhausting.

Ethan and I left the reception in his truck, which had been decorated with typical *Just Married* writing all over the windows. We were spending the night at a nearby resort, but he pulled into a car wash on the way there and cleaned off all of the writing so, as he said, it wouldn't *ruin the paint*. I was shocked he couldn't have waited to do this.

I should have realized this was just a sign of things to come.

We planned to have a nice dinner at the resort; and once in the room, I changed into a new white sundress I had purchased just for this occasion.

But when I put on my heeled sandals, I snagged one of them on a ruffle on the dress and tore off a large part of it. Although inconsequential in the big picture, I was devastated. I just sat on the bed and cried. I was so tired, and the stress of the entire weekend was now hitting me all at once.

I felt like I had been so rushed into trying to plan a wedding and make dresses, all while trying to graduate from college. I was also trying to spend a little time with my out-of-town family before the wedding; and now that it was over, I just wanted to relax and go to sleep for two days. Instead, I was getting dressed to go out to dinner for the first time as a married woman; and I had torn the only dress I brought with me for the weekend.

Ethan took me to a nearby drugstore, but the only thing I could find to repair my dress was a box of safety pins. I used them to pin together the tear on the backside of the ruffle and hoped the restaurant was dark enough that no one would notice *the girl in the torn dress*.

I can't even recall what we ate, but I remember going back to the room and falling fast asleep from the exhaustion of the entire semester. Needless to say, my first night as a newly married woman was hardly romantic.

Over the course of the next several weeks, nothing was much different then it had been before the wedding.

We were still living in the same apartment, but now; I was trying to find a job in Starkville. Ethan thought I should take just any retail sales job. "Everyone starts at the bottom," he told me. I explained to him that since I had just graduated from college with a degree in Fashion Merchandising, I was qualified to do more than just be a salesgirl.

I was still going to church alone every Sunday morning, and we spent every Sunday afternoon at Ethan's parent's house. After I returned from church, I would change my clothes; and we would drive up to Ethan's parents' house in West Point, about thirty to forty-five minutes away. We would have Sunday lunch with his parents and sister and hang out on their forty acres, hunting, canoeing and fishing or just target shooting most afternoons. I was never asked to help with preparing lunch and usually sat around reading things from a pile of junk mail stacked up on the coffee table. I was not comfortable in their home—it was not what I had been accustomed to growing up.

It was a ranch-style block home they had lived in for over 20 years, with three bedrooms and two bathrooms, but the master bathroom had never been finished; and so it was just a half bathroom. Everyone bathed in the full bathroom located in the hallway. There was an Arcadia door leading out into the backyard of the house, but no patio had ever been built onto the house; so there was a two to three foot drop off outside the door and the door was never used.

They entered the home through the garage, so the garage door was rarely closed; and the front door was never used. The front of the house, which was meant to be a living room and dining room, was just used for storage. Ethan's former bedroom was also used for storage, it had become the craft room.

I would not necessarily call these family members *hoarders* (I don't think that term was being used yet), but they had *a lot of stuff.*

Having had an interest in architecture and design, I was uncomfortable by the state of their house and disliked being there all day, every Sunday. I asked Ethan if I could clean and organize his parent's living room/dining room one day, as a gift, while his mom was at work; and he got mad at me. I wasn't going to throw stuff away, just organize it.

They were just so different from me and my family, it was difficult to be comfortable around them. His parents were nice to me, but we never became close; and we never just sat and talked. Even Ethan's older sister and I didn't talk much—and we were about the same age.

After we returned to Starkville on Sunday evenings, we would have dinner, which was usually leftovers from lunch; and we would watch television. I would then prepare Ethan's lunches for the following week before heading to bed.

We had only been married for about six weeks, when Ethan and I were playing cards one Saturday night, and he freaked out when I made a remark about my old boyfriends.

I'm not sure exactly what the comment was, but we had probably had a couple of beers; and I figured it didn't matter since we were now married, and he was the one I had chosen to spend my future with.

He stormed out of the living room and went into the bedroom and called Sally, complaining about me and my past boyfriends. I'm not sure why he wouldn't have called his best friend, Dave, to talk. Ethan must have thought he had been my first serious boyfriend, and wasn't happy there had been others before him. This didn't make sense to me because he knew about my past, and he knew I had given birth to a baby girl at the age of eighteen. He never seemed concerned with that, nor had he ever even asked me any details about her or about her biological father. Sally told him he was getting worked up over nothing and that she, too, had several serious boyfriends in her past.

He came back out into the living room, and said I wasn't the girl he thought I was; he felt that my mom had tricked him into marrying me when we weren't yet ready to get married because she was a religious freak.

He told me he wanted a divorce.

I tried to explain to Ethan that my past had nothing to do with our future—he was the one I had chosen to marry—he was the person I saw in my future. He said he did not see us together in the future. But in my mind, no matter how we had started out, marriage was supposed to be for life. I was committed to try to do all I could to hold ours together, but Ethan slept in the guest room that night; and the next day I woke up alone in our apartment.

Ethan had already taken off—somewhere—without even leaving a note.

If Ethan went to his parents' house that day, I'm not sure what he told them about why I wasn't with him—though he may not have even gone there. I got dressed for church and left the apartment; but when I returned, he still wasn't home, so I just hung out in our apartment and watched television.

I finally made his lunches for the week and got ready for bed. He showed up later in the evening and just sat in his recliner and watched television, and then he came to bed.

Nothing more was said about the divorce.

Chapter 13

Spinning my wheels

1983

Because most of the students had moved out of the apartments & condominiums that Ethan's dad owned at the end of the school year, they needed to be cleaned and painted before the students returned to school. I had started helping clean and paint after school ended and soon took over doing that full time, for a month or two. Ethan's dad would pay me cash for the hours I worked each week when we went to their house on Sundays. It was around Fall when his parents suggested it would be a good idea for us to move to West Point. Ethan was already working there and that would save him the drive to work each day. They suggested that I could apply for a job, working assembly at the Garanimals clothing factory; apparently, they didn't really understand how little that related to *Fashion Merchandising*. I chose to keep my mouth shut and remain the obedient, *Mississippi wife*.

There was a section of land on Ethan's parent's property that we began to clear, and the plan was to put a trailer on the property so we could move into it and live there. I hated the thought of living in a trailer, but agreed that maybe it was for the best.

Ethan said that maybe we could build a house on the property in the future, so that was a little more appealing.

While we were working on the land one day, I stepped on a branch and an extremely large thorn went through the heel of my sneaker and right into my foot. To me, it was a sign this was the last place I really wanted to live—or work. We had to drive home to Starkville and go to the clinic, where a tetanus shot was administered. Strangely, we never discussed moving to West Point again.

I often thought about my plans to move to the coast and design beach clothing and wondered how I had ended up so far away from that ambition.

I finally ended up being hired as an assistant manager for a small clothing store in the older part of downtown, but it didn't last long because of issues with my manager. I was being paid very little per hour, while she was on salary; but she spent most of her days shopping or going to lunch while I ran the store alone a lot of the time. She also had me doing all of the work she didn't want to do, like calling on the credit accounts, while she would hang out on the phone in the back room.

After being unemployed again for a short time, a friend who I had worked with in College, at the hotel bar near campus, called me and asked me if I wanted a job at a new club she was managing.

I was thrilled, and so was she—we had gotten along well together at work, and she knew that with my experience, I would require little training.

During my first night at my new job, I was having a great time and making good money. I loved being back in a club, with live music and crowds of people dancing. Ethan came into the club to *check it out* and all seemed fine—until we left the club.

Once home, he told me I was not going back to work there. When I asked him why not, he said he didn't like the way the other guys in the place were looking at me! I explained to him that it was just a job, and I made good money. No one had hit on me and besides, I always wore my wedding ring. He didn't care what I thought; he was jealous of anyone who even looked at me.

I realized this same thing had happened at least twice before while we were dating; once, when we were out dancing at a club, and another time, when we were out playing pool. Both times we had to leave because he was uncomfortable with other guys looking at me. At the time, his possessiveness had been somewhat flattering, but I should have realized it was an indication of a bigger problem; he was possessive, obsessive and paranoid.

It had even happened again, after we were married, when I was cleaning and painting apartments.

Some of the guys I knew from school hired me to clean their apartments and houses while they were in classes or working on their cars or other things. Ethan knew these guys and had partied with all of them, but suddenly one day, I was told I could no longer talk to them or clean their homes; because he knew they were all *after me.* It was all in his imagination—I had known these guys long before Ethan, and none of them had ever flirted with me since Ethan and I had started dating and especially not now that I was married. I really felt that Ethan didn't want me to have any independence.

I was stuck in a marriage that I had been trying to save, and I had no money with which to do anything else or go anywhere else.

One day, the new store manager, from the clothing store where I used to work downtown, called and wanted to know if I would like a temporary job, helping them set up their new store. The new manager had been hired to replace the one I had worked with, and the owners were modernizing their store and moving it out of the old downtown area. Finally, I had a chance at a real job back in the fashion industry. Ethan could not complain about this job—this was why I went to college.

After being in a *not so happy* marriage for the last year, stuck in a small town, with no possibilities of a career; I was actually excited to work in a clothing store again!

After helping the crew set everything up and putting up the new displays, they offered me the job of assistant manager. It wasn't as much money per hour as I had been making cleaning and painting apartments or waitressing, but it was more hours—nearly forty per week—and a permanent job —and the environment was much nicer.

Every weekday morning, I got up by 5:30 am and made Ethan's breakfast while he got ready for work. Then I put together his lunch, which was mostly pre-made on Sunday evenings.

After Ethan left, I would hang out in the recliner, watching television re-runs of "Bewitched" and "I Dream of Jeannie". Then I would get showered and dressed and leave for work, so I could be there by 9:30 am to open the store for the associates. I worked until the store closed at 6 pm and would usually be home by 6:30 pm. Sometimes Ethan would be home, sometimes he wouldn't be.

Because he usually got off work around 2:30 pm to 3 pm, he would meet up with his friends in West Point and go out fishing, or hunting, or who knows what. Most of the time, I would get dinner started so we could eat around 7 pm—if Ethan had come home in time to shower before then.

One evening, I walked in the door from work later than usual; and Ethan was sitting in his recliner, already showered and changed from work, watching television.

He asked me, "What's for dinner?" I told him I hadn't planned dinner yet. I was angry that he had probably been home for hours and hadn't even started dinner. But he was angry with me because I was late, and he thought I should have started something before I left for work. "What do you do all morning, after I leave for work?"

That was it for me. I told him he could start making dinner if he got home from work before I did, and he could get up early and make his own breakfasts too. He thought I should do it all. *His mother had raised two children and cooked all their family meals and taken care of their house, why couldn't I do the same?* Well, his mother might have raised two children and cooked all their meals, but she didn't work until after her kids were in school, and our apartment was a heck of a lot cleaner than their house.

While I stood there faced with just how much of a *Mama's boy* he was, I realized it was a good thing we hadn't decided to have children of our own yet.

I couldn't do it all, and I didn't want to; especially for someone who didn't appreciate what I did do and was always telling me I was doing something wrong. I did the best I could.

In September, the day before my twenty-fourth birthday started like any other day. I watched television while I ate breakfast, cleaned up the kitchen, showered and dressed, and left for work.

153

Since it was a Saturday, I assumed Ethan had made plans to go hunting or fishing with his friends for the day. In the back of my mind, I was thinking that maybe we would go out to dinner for my birthday that evening when I got home. But when I arrived home from work, a different kind of birthday surprise was waiting for me—Ethan had moved out of our apartment!

I found a note, telling me that he had rented a small trailer on the country road on his route to work. He told me he thought this was for the best, as things never worked out like *we* had planned. He also said he would be filing for divorce. I was stunned. What would I do now? I had tried to work things out in my marriage; and in the process, I had lost several friends and jobs and a chance at a career.

I was stuck in Starkville and had very little money. I only cleared close to five hundred dollars a month, of which a huge chunk went for gas in my Impala just to get back and forth to work. Now, I would have to pay more than half of my take-home pay in rent and utilities, which meant there was very little left over for food, clothing or other necessities. To make matters worse, I had no real furniture, other than my old mattress and dresser. Thankfully, I still had my stereo—music had always helped me through the hard times. Music brought me comfort when I was a single pregnant teen, it kept me entertained through two different Colleges; and it would kept me company, now that I was alone in my apartment.

Once again, my life was in limbo, and I wasn't sure what I should do. For the time being, I figured since I finally had a decent job; I would stay in the apartment and try to find a roommate.

I had become friends with one of the girls at work, Lily, a high school senior who worked at the store part-time; and so I reached out to her for comfort. Although I was her manager, neither of us let that become an issue. She came over with a bottle of wine from her parents' stash that night; and we celebrated my birthday, sitting on the floor, listening to *Heart*. Luckily, our store was closed on Sundays. Lily was the only child of upper class parents and had everything she could ever need or want, she only worked at our store to get a discount on clothing. She offered to loan me a television, but I told her I couldn't really afford the cable bill anyway; so I would just listen to music on my stereo.

I spent the next week looking for furniture. I couldn't afford much, so I decided to build a shelving unit from some fruit crates I collected from the grocery store. I went home to the Academy for a day and Edward helped me put it together in the wood shop. He had moved home, after graduating from college, to work at the Academy.

Once set up in the apartment, I placed my collection of seashells on top of it. This display made me feel much more comfortable in my surroundings.

I still hadn't made it back to the beach-other than a long weekend Ethan and I took once, so he could check out the job situation. Recalling that trip made me realize he never really intended on moving to the coast—it was just too far away from his family and friends and hunting and fishing.

Now that my display shelf was put together and in place, I bought a wicker *love-seat* from a small shop next to my clothing store. It wasn't much, but it was on sale, and at least I had something I could sit on—besides the floor. I was able to fit the *love-seat* in the backseat of my Impala-which was even more convenient. Unfortunately, I couldn't afford the extra cushion for it at the time; but I knew I could use my sewing machine and design skills to make one in the future.

The furniture store, next to the store where I worked, was owned by two brothers. They were both attractive—and blonde—and reminded me of Florida surfers. I couldn't afford to take myself out to eat lunch during the workdays any longer, so I often spent my lunch breaks in their store, just looking around.

Ethan had been gone for a little over a month when the younger of the two brothers, Brad, asked me if I wanted to go out with him after work one evening to get something to eat; I said yes. It sounded innocent enough.

Their store stayed open longer than ours, so I offered to meet him somewhere.

He said he would like to pick me up, so I didn't have to use all the gas up in my car, driving back across town. This was fine by me, and so we made plans for the following Saturday evening. When he showed up at my door, I wasn't quite finished getting ready. I asked him to have a seat, on the love-seat I had purchased from his store. He laughed at how uncomfortable the love-seat was without a cushion on it, and I told him I planned on making one soon. I went back into the bathroom to finish my makeup and hair.

When the phone rang, I still had curlers in my hair; so I asked Brad if he wouldn't mind answering it. He told me the caller just hung up on him. I laughed and told him it was probably a wrong number. When the phone rang a second time, I answered it and was taken aback to hear Ethan's voice on the other end of the line. He immediately asked me who had answered the phone the first time he called; and I told him it was just a friend of mine, as I had been in the bathroom when it rang. Ethan said there had been some burglaries in the area recently, and he was just checking on me to make sure I was all right. He had left behind a forty-five caliber hand gun, which I had proclaimed I did not need and would probably not use; but he convinced me I should have it for my personal safety. He told me if my life was in danger, I most likely wouldn't have any problem using it.

I wondered why he even cared, being that he had no shame in having left me alone in the first place.

Brad and I left and went to dinner at a popular fast food restaurant in town, during which I made it clear that I did not consider this outing a *date*, as I was still legally married. He told me he enjoyed my company and would be happy to just be my friend. He was tired of eating all his meals alone or with his brother.

When we got back to my apartment, I invited Brad in to listen to some live music I had recorded from a radio show. I was happy to be spending time with someone in Mississippi who was not just a country music fan. But when we entered the apartment, a feeling came over me that something was not right. A light was now on in my bedroom, which I was certain I had turned off. I checked both bedrooms, closets, and the bathroom, as Brad just stood near the front door. I also verified the gun was where I kept it. Other than the light, nothing else seemed to be out of place; but when I returned to the living room, I noticed a pair of Ethan's boots on the floor behind the front door.

The realization had both of us nervous, and so I called Ethan and asked him why he had been in my apartment and why had he left a pair of his boots by the front door?

"I just wanted to remind you that I still have a key, and we are still married." This, to me, was such a creepy thing for someone to do; it really scared me, and I felt that he could come back at any time.

I didn't want to get into an argument with him over the phone, especially not in front of Brad; but I reminded him that *he* had left me and told me *he* was filing for a divorce.

"I'm not your property and you can't tell me what I can and can't do," I said, as I hung up the phone.

It was no surprise that Brad decided to leave. I told him I understood and that would probably be for the best. He never asked me out again, and I could hardly blame him.

Ethan had left me, asked me for a divorce, and had moved out of my life; yet now I had lost another friend because of his behavior.

I soon learned from Ethan that his Dad had recently sold the two apartment buildings he owned, one of them just happened to be the one in which I was living. The new owner was going to be raising the rent, and I still hadn't found a roommate.

By mid-November, I'd been two months on my own without a roommate and could no longer afford to keep my apartment. I informed Ethan that I was going to have to move to a smaller place—and to my surprise, he asked me to move in with him.

He told me he had two furnished bedrooms, and I could have my own room; and his rent was so cheap, I wouldn't have to pay anything.

159

He knew how much I hated the thought of living in a trailer, and I didn't even have the address of where the trailer was that he lived in; so I didn't know how bad it was going to be.

When I finally went over to see the trailer, it was old and scary; if you opened the cabinet under the bathroom sink, you could see the ground underneath it! But the reality of my financial situation over-ruled my apprehension, and hoping this would be a temporary solution, I agreed to the move. I suppose, in the back of my mind, I also thought maybe God was giving me an opportunity to work things out with my estranged husband. And then during our discussions, Ethan told me he wanted to remain friends no matter how things ended up, but he, too, had hoped perhaps we could save our marriage.

One day, while home, packing up my stuff to move out of the apartment, my phone rang; and again, it was Thomas. *He had the strangest way of showing up in my life, just when I needed a friend to talk to.*

He told me that he had just come across my phone number and had been thinking about me, wondering how I was doing now and how married life was. He said he had been afraid to call me, not knowing who would answer the phone. I explained to him that Ethan and I had actually been separated for a few months but were now going to try to work things out, and I was moving back in with him.

"Is that really what you want to do?" he asked. I'm certain he sensed my hesitation. "Yes, I think I should give our marriage another try." I replied. Thomas always seemed to know me better than I knew myself. My sister, Leigh, had been asking me the same question recently.

My double mattress ended up back at my mother's apartment, and I was now relegated to a twin bed in the *extra room*—well, at least *most* of the time. For the most part, things were going pretty well, but I still wasn't *allowed* to spend time with any of my old friends because of Ethan's jealousy.

Looking back, Ethan had probably only moved me into the trailer with him so he could keep an eye on me. He didn't want me to spend time with any of my friends, let alone have the opportunity to date anyone.

I decided to fly to Ohio with Edward to visit my Dad, which had become a Thanksgiving tradition since my parents' divorce. Although our Dad was still in treatment for his cancer, he seemed to be doing okay.

He surprised us by having, Leigh, and her new husband, Rick, fly into town, on their way home from Europe. We were all astonished when Leigh stepped through the gate at the airport, obviously pregnant; and she told us she was six months along.

She was turning thirty at the end of that month; and after struggling through a few bad relationships of her own, this was going to be a first for Leigh—and the rest of the family. A new baby was entering all of our lives and this was cause for celebration.

I suppose, technically, I had produced the first grandchild, but my family never talked about that.

Leigh knew of the trouble I had been having with Ethan. She asked me if I was interested in becoming their *au pair*, and helping them out with the baby. I told her that I had recently moved back in with Ethan and we were trying to work things out. "Do you really want to work things out with Ethan?" she asked. "Do you really want to stay in Mississippi, or raise a family with a man who has caused you so much unhappiness?" I told her at the time, I felt like trying to work things out with Ethan was the right thing to do.

After I returned to Mississippi, Leigh began calling me at work, weekly, on my manager's day off. I would be in the back room, working on payroll and eating a bag of Brach's chocolates (one of my few stress relievers); and she would grill me on whether I would still consider becoming their nanny. She and Rick had determined they were definitely going to hire someone to help them with their baby, and she had thought her sister would be the best person for the job.

Their baby was due in March, and they lived in California, where she claimed the weather was always warm!

I told her Ethan and I were still working on our relationship, and things seemed to be going well. Since Christmas was coming up soon, I also told her perhaps once the holidays were over, I'd have a clearer picture of our future together.

That conversation would come back to haunt me.

On Christmas Eve, Ethan and I sat near the small tree he had cut from his parent's property and exchanged gifts. When I opened Ethan's, I was touched by the beautiful, wooden box, with a carved heart on the front of it. I opened the box to look inside, and what did I find?

Not jewelry—I slowly unfolded the papers—not a love letter or a poem—but divorce papers!

I was outraged! My body and mind were so stressed that I didn't even know how to react, and I could barely think straight. Why had he waited until I had moved back in with him to do this? I stood up and went to *my* room where I sat down and wrote a long letter to Leigh. I wished I could have talked to her instead, but I knew she and Rick were spending the holidays in their cabin in Rio Nido, in Northern California. I didn't have a telephone number for them at the cabin, but my letter would be waiting for her when she returned home.

I knew I would spend the next week at work, waiting for her to call me. I told her in the letter that I had decided I would move to California after all.

Ethan and I each spent Christmas day at our own parent's houses, not together, as a married couple. I mailed the letter to Leigh the day after Christmas, and strangely enough, I received a letter from her just a couple of days later; they must have crossed in the mail. She had written the letter to me while they were at their cabin.

She asked me how things were working out with Ethan, and she asked me to reconsider their offer. She told me I would be paid well and would be able to travel with the three of them. She also asked me to commit for just six months; if I wanted to return to work in retail fashion after that, I would certainly have more opportunities to do so in California, than in Mississippi.

Receiving her letter was a big relief.

I told Ethan I would sign the divorce papers and would be moving to California.

We somehow parted as friends and went together to have the divorce paperwork signed and notarized. Maybe it was a sign meant to tell me I was making the right move, because a few weeks before I quit my job, we had a horrible blizzard.

We were left without electricity and had to bring the large mattress off Ethan's bed into the living room so we could sleep in the living room, near the kitchen and the gas stove for heat. Ethan hung a heavy blanket over the hallway entrance to keep the cold from seeping back into the living room.

We took the little bit of food we had out of the refrigerator and left it out on the front steps to stay cold. We kept an ear to our portable radio, and the public was advised that most businesses were closed, and people should stay inside —unless it was an emergency. When we ran out of food, we deemed it an emergency and headed into town in Ethan's four-wheel drive pick-up truck.

The roads were covered in ice; the town was mostly deserted, but the convenience store up the hill was open, though nearly empty. We were just glad that it was even open and someone was working. We bought a few food items; soup, instant hot chocolate, and a box of Twinkies. The eggs, milk, and bread were already sold out. We returned to the trailer to warm up. As it turned out, body heat happened to be the best way to keep warm.

The storm passed, and I returned to my store to finish up my last few weeks of work. For the first time in a long while, I was beginning to feel optimistic about my future, not to mention leaving the cold and going to California— where I hoped my beloved sun would be shining.

I packed my clothes into two large boxes I got from our store, and I gave Lily my stereo to hold for me. Strangely enough, she didn't have a stereo in her bedroom, only a radio/alarm clock. I planned to take my car back to my mom's apartment at the Academy, and asked her if she would try to sell it for me. I told her in the meantime, she could drive it, if needed. I also asked her if she would hold my other things in storage at her apartment until I decided if I was going to stay in California or not.

By the next weekend, I had everything packed, my bank account was closed, my mail was forwarded—and I realized I hadn't had my period yet. Between working and packing and all of the stress of the divorce, I couldn't even remember when it was due. As if things hadn't been complicated enough, an unplanned pregnancy now would have been devastating.

I made an appointment to see my Doctor at the campus clinic and filled her in on what was going on. I'd been seeing her for years, and she knew my entire history. She had suggested that I go on birth control pills in College to regulate my periods and had continued refilling my prescription after I got married, knowing we hadn't planned on having children anytime soon.

"You probably should have gone back on the pill when you moved back in with Ethan," she told me. "I never planned on going off of them," I replied.

"I only quit refilling them to save money when he gave me divorce papers as a Christmas gift!" I explained to her the only time we had been together since Christmas, had been during the blizzard.

"It only takes once!" she remarked. As if anyone needed to remind me of that.

To my great relief, the pregnancy test was negative. But it was a stark reminder that I was still not ready to raise a child. It had been over six years since I'd given my baby girl up for adoption. I'd graduated from college, worked several jobs and tried to start a career; I'd been married and was about to be divorced.

I was twenty-four years old; I may have had more life experiences, but I still wasn't mature enough or financially stable enough to be a great mom.

Perhaps spending time as a nanny would help to move me in that direction in the future.

Chapter 14

California, Here I Come

1985

My trip to California began at a tiny airport near Starkville. The first half of my trip would be on a very small plane, which would take me to Texas. Ethan took me to the airport with a couple of our friends, Ethan's best friend, Dave, and his girlfriend, Debbie. I was terrified to fly in such a little plane, and shared with everyone how I was feeling. During our goodbye drinks at the airport, Debbie gave me a little something she had leftover from a dental surgery to help me relax on the flight. I hugged Ethan goodbye and told him to call me at Leigh's house, anytime, if he had any questions and to let me know when the divorce was final.

From Texas, I flew to Oakland, and Leigh and Rick were at the airport to pick me up. When Rick saw my two large boxes on the carousel, he told me they weren't going to fit in his car; and he'd have to come back the next day to pick them up in his stepfather's pickup truck.

It was a little disconcerting to leave what few things I had brought with me (besides my carry-on) at an airport.

The next morning, I ended riding with Rick's stepdad, back to the airport to get my boxes.

Thankfully, they were stored in a small room with several other pieces of abandoned luggage.

Leigh and I spent that afternoon talking and catching up and watching *Guiding Light,* while I unpacked my stuff. She showed me the rest of the house and the pool deck where she spent a lot of time; although I thought it was still a little too cool to be sunbathing, being as it was only the beginning of March.

The second day I was in California, Leigh and I just hung out at the house again; but late in the afternoon, her water broke and she went into labor (at two weeks over due, she'd received a little help from castor oil and Cognac). Rick came home and casually had a quick meal; while I thought they should leave right away, knowing our family seemed to have a history of quick labor and delivery.

The birthing center was a private facility, complete with a midwife; and it was in San Francisco, about an hour away from their house.

Later that evening, Rick called to tell me that my nephew, Jordan, had arrived into the world and everyone was doing well. I was alone at my new home, not knowing anyone and wondering what I should do until they came back home —which would mostly likely be at least another day. I stayed up late and watched television and then had a hard time sleeping, in a strange place, alone.

The next morning, I was in the kitchen, just staring out the window in wonderment at the extraordinary view across the street. Their house was built into the side of a hill in San Leandro; and when I stepped out the front door, the first thing I noticed was a grazing deer, off in the distance. We were in the middle of suburbia and there was a deer, grazing on the hill, above the houses! When I turned around to go back into the house, I realized, to my dismay; the door had locked itself behind me.

I panicked!

I didn't know anyone, and Leigh and Rick were still in a birthing center in San Francisco. I had no way to reach them and spent the next twenty minutes looking for a hidden spare key, with no luck.

"Hey, Eliza!" I said out loud. "You're not in Mississippi anymore!" Apparently, folks in California didn't leave extra keys under their front door mats or hidden in planters.

I looked around and saw a man in his garage across the street. I knew Rick had lived in the house for several years; so I assumed, *hoped*, he would be friends with the neighbors. I tentatively crossed the street and approached the man in the garage. I explained my predicament, and I'm certain it was my resemblance to my sister that convinced him I was telling the truth. Thankfully, he happened to have the names and phone number of Rick's parents.

I looked up and said my thanks; once again, God seeming to be looking out for me. The neighbor let me use his phone to make the call, and Rick's dad agreed to drive over to the house with his spare key. I was thankful he was retired and didn't mind me giving him things to do to keep him busy.

Rick called from the birthing center later that day and told me he would be staying the night with Leigh and Jordan, and the three of them would be home the next afternoon. I spent the rest of the day doing laundry and straightening up in preparation for their return home.

I was thrilled to have some free time, with no real work, to park myself in front of a television and watch *Guiding Light* and a few other shows.

The next day, I officially became a nanny.

I spent the next several months helping Leigh and Rick care for my nephew. We traveled often; short trips to Sonoma County, Lake Tahoe, or Santa Cruz and much longer trips to places like Palm Springs and even Hawaii.

I especially loved the trip to Hawaii, because we traveled to three different Islands; and with Jordan being only three months old at the time, I had a chance to go out a couple of nights with guys I met while I was there. I even considered moving to Maui or Kauai after my six months of being a nanny had expired, but I just didn't have the nerve to do it.

Hawaii was so far away; and I really would have had to start all over in a career there, and it was quite expensive to live in Hawaii. It was tempting though, since I would no longer have any family responsibilities on the mainland and no commitments to anyone.

I really loved taking care of my nephew. He was such a mellow child and so content to lie in his crib, watching his mobile and listening to it play music above him. He only cried when he was hungry, and that is when Leigh took him, most of the time, as she was breastfeeding—when she was home. When Leigh and Rick would go out in the evenings, Jordan and I would sing and dance around the living room to my albums, playing on their stereo.

It was a great way to make a living, but when Jordan slept, Rick often gave me tasks to do or asked me to come to work in his office.

Working at his office though gave me an opportunity to make new friends; and I got to know a couple of girls, who invited me to go out with them when I had a weekend night off, and we stayed in town. Sometimes we would go to the theatre or a movie, but more often we would go out to a club to dance.

I met a guy named James at the restaurant/nightclub we frequented. He was one of the bartenders and eventually, we became friends.

172

After six months of working as a nanny, I told Leigh and Rick I was ready to return to working in retail and fashion, and I had applied for a job at a nearby mall. I was hired as a co-manager of Limited Express, and I typically worked mostly day shifts, though I worked until after 9 pm one or two nights each week.

I started out having to take a bus to/from the mall where I worked—which I hated doing—but I could only do this during the day shifts. Leigh would take me to and pick me up from the bus station when I worked the night shifts—but I hated doing that also—so, after about a week, I purchased an old Volvo from Rick's mom, financed by my father (when the bank turned me down for a car loan).

Now, when I worked the early shift, I would go to the club after work and eat for free from the buffet during Happy Hour and dance with some of the *regulars*. There was a particular group of male school teachers who would meet me there on the weekends and buy me glasses of wine in return for my assistance in helping them find dance partners. Most of the guys at the club thought James and I were dating, and so they didn't flirt with me; but they did hang out with me while James was working. James lived near me, with his dad, and did not own a car; so I often offered to give him rides home from the club if he would get me into the club for free on weekends.

Rents were high in California, so I continued to live with Leigh and Rick; but I started paying them for my room, still helping to babysit when I could. I was still struggling financially; my retail salary was barely enough to pay all my bills, including rent to Rick, my car payment to my Dad, my student loan, new clothes at my store, *and* going out at night—let alone affording my own place in California.

When James told me he was going to move to Arizona to help open a new location for his restaurant chain, I told him that I was ready to move too.

Chapter 15

Back to the desert

1986

I'd always wanted to go back to see where it was I had started my life, in Arizona. I was sure I could transfer with my job; so I made the request, and it was approved. It was not the exact location I had hoped for, but it was still in the same city. I told James I was set to transfer and would be moving to Phoenix at the end of January. James' transfer wasn't going to happen until the end of February though. "I will go on ahead and try to find a place for us to live," I told him. In the meantime, I hoped I would be able to afford an apartment by myself, if needed.

Through a friend of Rick's, I ended up making plans to temporarily share a two bedroom apartment with the man's son, whom I had met during our trip to Santa Cruz. But before I left California, I found out he had rented the room to someone else. He told me that his sister, Kris, had an apartment across the walkway from his; and she too, needed a roommate. I recalled meeting her as well and remembered that she seemed to be a very immature eighteen-year old. But at the time, I didn't have any other choices, so I agreed to share her apartment with her until James arrived; and we found a place of our own to rent.

My last night in Northern California I spent at the club, dancing with and saying goodbye to my friends. I had been to my favorite salon and experimented with a new *messy-layered* haircut—scrunched, with plenty of hair gel. I had also purchased an awesome black cotton lace dress that reminded me of something Stevie Nicks would have worn, complete with black lace pumps. I was back into a size seven—I guess snacking all day and dancing all night had it's advantages. I got very little sleep that night but woke early to load up my Volvo. At noon, I said goodbye to Rick, Leigh, and Jordan and began what I thought would be about an eighteen hour trip to Phoenix.

I made it as far as Southern California, and my car started to overheat while driving through the mountains. I kept pulling over on the side of the highway, in the dark, adding water to the radiator. It wasn't until well after nightfall that I found a twenty-four hour repair shop. The night manager was nice enough to replace my thermostat at a reasonable price and offered to do it while I waited.

I didn't feel comfortable though, hanging out in an auto repair shop at night and was relieved when I was finally back on the road. By that time though, I was exhausted and didn't feel it was safe to keep driving until I could get a couple hours of sleep. I considered sleeping in my car at the next rest stop, but it happened to be filled with 18-wheelers, which seemed less safe than driving tired.

Instead, I found a nice little motel, close to the highway, where I was able to sleep for a few hours and get showered. Neither the car repair or the motel had been factored into my budget, and my savings account was becoming quickly depleted. But I had a tax refund check coming, which would be forwarded by Leigh to the apartment I was going to share with Kris. Knowing I would have that check arriving for me soon after I got to Phoenix, eased my concerns. It would be a couple more weeks before I received a full paycheck from my new job.

Kris was expecting me to arrive between 6am and noon, so I was on the road again by 6am.

Once I entered Phoenix, I ended up on the Southwest side of town, which was inhabited primarily by the Hispanic community. I was having a hard time finding my destination; but when I stopped to ask for help, everyone I came across spoke Spanish—and I didn't speak a word of Spanish. (I actually never thought I would live in the Southwest and had hoped to be traveling to Europe in the future to visit a cousin who lived there, and so I learned French when I was in high school.)

I finally found a very nice bilingual woman who explained to me that the "I-17" I was looking for was also called "Black Canyon freeway" and told me how to access it. I drove north; but by the time I exited the freeway, I was thinking that maybe I should have stayed in California.

There were businesses and apartment buildings everywhere and no greenery at all. I guess I had become spoiled living with Rick and Leigh, traveling to nice places in the mountains of California and living in one of the most beautiful states in the country. Phoenix was not at all what I was expecting.

Thankfully, the further I drove east, the more affluent the neighborhoods looked.

To my relief, I finally found the apartment complex. Though an older complex, it was a quaint little residence with two, long, single-story buildings. There was a walkway and appealing foliage in between them. I pulled into a guest parking space and walked around to the center walkway to find my apartment number. It was just past noon, and I was certain my new roommate would be wondering where I was by then.

It took several knocks on the door before my roommate answered. When she did so, she told me her parents were still sleeping. Apparently, they had spent the night in the room that was to be mine because they were having their house painted. My new roommate actually asked me if I could come back in an hour!

This was mind boggling to me. After having driven all the way to Phoenix from San Leandro, on four hours of sleep; now I was supposed to leave my new home and come back later, so as not to inconvenience her parents?

Where was I supposed to go with a car piled full with all of my belongings (and little extra cash) in a strange town?

Unfortunately, these were the first indications of things to come.

I drove to the closest 7-11 and splurged to buy a diet Pepsi and a map of the city. I needed to figure out where I was and how to get to my new job the next day. When I returned to the apartment, I gave Kris one week's rent for January, even though it was already the end of the month, and a thirty day deposit. I intended for her to use that deposit when I gave her my notice, which I hoped would be by the middle of the following month, and moved out.

Kris gave me a key to the front door, but said she didn't have an extra mailbox key and promised she would check the mail each day when she was home and give me any mail that was for me. I unloaded my car without any offer of help from my new roommate.

I had told Kris previously I didn't own a bed, and she told me she had an extra mattress in the spare room. I was surprised to find that her parents had taken it with them that day when they left. Did they think I could somehow transport a mattress from California to Arizona in a Volvo? Kris told me they probably had an extra one I could use, and she would ask them.

In the meantime, I told her I would try to sleep on my wicker love seat, which I had shipped from Mississippi to California, (along with my antique rocking chair and my china and crystal). Luckily, I was able to ship them again from California to Arizona and they should be arriving soon.

Kris soon departed, saying she had errands to run for her family's business. I couldn't help but wonder what kind of business errands needed to be run on a Sunday.

Over the course of the next few days, I learned that Kris' family had lost their beautiful house in Santa Cruz (that they had totally renovated) the previous year and moved to Phoenix, intending on starting their own real estate development company in Arizona. Both of the adult children worked for the family business and used roommates to help pay for their apartments. But, within two weeks of living with Kris, I was ready to move on.

I had gone to the manager's apartment to pay my half of the rent on the first Friday of February and found out that Kris was trying to charge me three quarters of the rental fee. While she stayed in the larger master bedroom with a private bathroom and patio, I got the extra room with all of her guests using my bathroom in the hallway. Additionally, one of her *out of town* boyfriends stayed with her almost every night but never contributed to the expenses.

To add to that, anytime I brought food home and had leftovers, someone else would eat them.

Kris was only working part time, running errands for her parents' business, and stayed home the rest of the time, renting and watching movies and doing numerous small loads of laundry—which only ran up the electric bill. She ate my food, and spent her money on designer clothes—or borrowed mine, without asking, when I wasn't at home.

When I learned James would be arriving by the beginning of March (and after only two weeks in Arizona), I told Kris I would be moving out and to consider this my thirty day notice. I also told her I wanted her to return all of the things she had *borrowed* from me.

She claimed she didn't have any of my stuff; and also determined that since I had not paid a security deposit for the electric bill, she needed me to do so now. I assumed she had spent my deposit on all the new designer clothing she was wearing. I told her she didn't need to worry about me paying my part of the electric bill when it arrived and explained that I had a full time job and another paycheck coming soon. I also told her since her parents were friends with my family, I would never leave without paying my financial obligations.

But I did tell Kris I would be paying only a third of the electric bill, not half, because she'd had numerous people staying in the apartment the entire time I had lived there.

By this time, I was actually in a bit of a financial bind. I had not yet received my tax refund check, and I was using my Sears charge card to buy snacks for lunch from their store in the mall where I worked. I explained to my Dad that I would have to delay my next car payment to him.

My dad generously offered to help me out by just giving me the car and forgiving any future payments. He'd helped Edward in the past to acquire a vehicle and wanted to do the same for me. I was extremely thankful for his help.

After my conversation with Kris, I tried to buy a lock for my bedroom door, but I couldn't find one I could afford. I started keeping all of my belongings inside of my bedroom, including my soap, shampoo and towels (more things Kris had been *borrowing*). Before I left for work each morning, I locked my door from the inside and climbed out the window. Not an optimal situation, but under the circumstances, it seemed the wisest thing to do. The downside was I had to sneak back into my own room every night.

It took Kris a while to figure out what I was doing.

In the beginning, I came in through the window and quietly unlocked my bedroom door and then went back outside and entered through the front door. But if it was late, I just came in through my window and went to bed.

Kris and her boyfriend finally figured out how I was getting into my room with the door locked and most likely, had been snooping around while I was at work. When they questioned me about my locked door, I played dumb and told them I only locked my door at night. I was floored when more of my belongings started to disappear. They were actually coming into my bedroom through my window, while I was at work, to take my belongings!

When my engagement ring from Ethan disappeared, I'd finally had it—I went to Kris' brother—since we were still friends—and told him what had been going on with his sister, and he suggested I discuss it with his mom. Since his mom was a friend of Leigh's, I felt like I could talk to her as one adult to another, and she agreed to help me get all of my things back. She also told me that she knew her daughter had problems, and I had not been the first roommate to move out after only a month.

I still hadn't received my tax refund, so I contacted the IRS to find out when it was mailed, and verified they now had my correct address. I explained to them that I was moving and didn't have a forwarding address yet. They informed me that I should have already received the check and offered to cancel the one that had been mailed to me. They said that a new check could be sent to me once I had my new address to give to them. I had a feeling the check had already come, but Kris had failed to give it to me.

By that time, I was hoping she had taken it and would get caught trying to cash it—that girl needed help.

When James finally arrived, I was so happy to see a friendly face. We added my belongings to his U-haul and found a place to sleep for the night. His job was paying for his moving expenses, so we didn't have to worry about spending money on a hotel until we found an apartment. We sat together with a free apartment guide I had picked up and spent the evening picking out places for us to look at the next day.

James was going to be working on the East side of town, in Scottsdale; and I was currently working on the West side of town, at a mall called Metro Center. I was hoping to be transferred to our Paradise Valley store, which was presently in between James new job and my current one, but that was still uncertain. James and I spent the next day driving around the Northeast end of the city, using my map to find our way, and settled on a place that was between Metro Center and the restaurant in Scottsdale.

Unfortunately, we had to wait for the manager to return from lunch to even see the apartment. It was only the first week of March; but sitting around outside, waiting for her to return, the heat was already getting to us. I had lived in Northern California for the last year, and James had lived there his entire life, so we were not used to such extreme heat so early in the year.

After the manager returned, we told her we wanted to lease a two-bed, two-bath apartment; but we were told the only ones available were in the family section, toward the back of the complex. We hadn't made it to view the available apartment yet when we realized this section of the complex was full of screaming kids. This wasn't going to work. Neither one of us wanted to be around a bunch of children at the time, so we told the manager we needed something in the adult only section of the complex. The manager said she only had a one-bed, one-bath apartment available in the adult only section. She questioned why we needed a two bedroom place, assuming we were a couple. I realize now that she was actually probably verifying we were the only two people who were going to be living in the apartment.

We explained that we were only friends and so had planned on renting a two bedroom apartment; but being that it was the only apartment available, and there was no way I would even consider staying another minute with Kris, we went ahead and signed a lease. It wasn't as though I had any furniture anyway. I figured I could just sleep on a couch in the living room. The closet in the bedroom was plenty big for two, and we determined that it could be shared. James had a bed and a dresser that he put in the bedroom, and we put his television in the living room. We went to the mall, and I used my Sears charge card to purchase a sofa-bed with a double size mattress.

We were able to take the sofa home in the U-haul before James returned it the next day, and a couple of guys in the complex offered to help us get it into the apartment. I also charged my new sheets and pillows; so other than a kitchen table and chairs, between the two of us, we had almost everything we needed. I was just happy not to be sleeping on my wicker love seat or a mattress on the floor again.

Our arrangement was great; James took care of the rent; and I paid the electric bill, the phone bill, and made sure the refrigerator was stocked with James' favorite things—Pepsi and peanut butter. He ate most of his meals at the restaurant the nights he worked. He went out with friends when he was off work or would fly to Vegas. We rarely ran in to each other—unless we both had the same days off—which was rare—so it was a great arrangement.

Except, when my mom came through town on her way to California to visit Leigh and Jordan and she stopped to visit me for a couple of days, she didn't understand why I had a male roommate. I explained to her our living arrangement, but she wouldn't stay there with me; and we had to find her a hotel for a couple of nights.

But I only had one day off work while she was in town, so we dealt with it.

Chapter 16

Another new beginning

1986

My arrangement with James worked well for several months. By summer, James was dating the restaurant owner's daughter, and I was dating our next door neighbor, Wayne. It was a good thing I didn't have many bills because by summer, I was also laid off. (The downfall of working in retail and getting a new area manager!)

James suggested I get a part time job at the restaurant where he worked; and so I ended up working part time during the weekdays at Bobby McGee's, answering phones and taking reservations.

"Thank you for calling Bobby McGee's, this is Goldilocks, how may I help you?" was engraved in my brain for months. It was only thirty hours per week, but with so few bills, I still had enough money to live on; and by now, Wayne was paying for a lot of my food, drinks, and entertainment.

By mid summer, James told me he had been asked to go back to San Francisco at the end of August to help open another new restaurant. The restaurant manager told me that things were slowing down for the summer months and offered me a new position, working for James until he left.

But I didn't want to work for James, so I considered returning to retail or possibly working as a live in nanny again, which would include room and board. I had really enjoyed working as a nanny for my nephew and wondered if I'd feel the same about working for a stranger.

But I hesitated considering a nanny position, because that meant I would have to move, and I was now spending most of my free time with Wayne. I ended up collecting unemployment for the next two months and spent most of my days out by the pool.

Wayne and I seemed like the perfect couple to most of our friends. He was my blonde surfer type and loved the beach and hanging out by the pool. We went to clubs and listened to music, and he even danced with me. He had a good job with the City of Phoenix and got up each weekday and went to work—unless we went to a concert—then he took time off the next day, since he had accrued plenty of paid hours. He also put in for overtime whenever possible, so he made good money. The one big downfall, at the time, was that he had an Ex wife and a two year old son.

Wayne didn't have regular visitation with his son; but I had seen his Ex wife and son visit him when I first moved into the apartment, before we started dating. I had never dated someone who was divorced, let alone with a child; so I was very hesitant about this being a long term relationship.

When I told Wayne I wasn't sure what I was going to do when James moved back to San Francisco, he mentioned that his lease was almost up; perhaps we could be roommates. He told me he was tired of *friends* crashing on his couch, not paying rent, and not cleaning up after themselves; and he determined I would make a great roommate.

We were spending most of our free time together by now, so it made sense; although I wasn't sure where this relationship was headed. We arranged with the apartment complex office for Wayne to break his current lease a month early and enter a new one with me when James moved out.

Before Wayne moved, his parents came to visit him from Northern Arizona. He told them the next time they came to visit, to just knock on the door next to his; because he would soon be moving over there to share my apartment with me!

This was the weirdest way I had ever been introduced to someone's parents.

Now that living arrangements were set, I spent the rest of the summer by the pool, pondering what I should do for work when my unemployment ran out.

At the end of August, James moved out and Wayne moved in.

I found a job at the grocery store bakery down the street from our apartment. It worked out well because the head baker allowed me to make up the schedule—and most of the time, Wayne and I worked the same schedules. I would meet Wayne at the bar next door to the grocery store, so we could have drinks at the end of our work days.

By the time Thanksgiving came around, my dad was sick again and having another surgery. I gave notice at the bakery and left to go to Ohio to visit him.

Wayne paid the rent; and with the few bills I had, I figured I could easily replace my income when I returned from Ohio. This way I would not have to worry about leaving my Dad to return to Phoenix because of work—like I had before. My Dad had surgery while I was visiting but seemed to be doing better afterwards.

I didn't really know all the details of what was going on with him—we were still not very close. I knew he had cancer and that it had spread, but I was under the impression that all the treatments and surgeries he had already endured helped him recover from this terrible disease.

While I was alone in his duplex, staying in my dad's old room; I found some old letters in the built in dresser drawer of his old bedroom—my guest room.

One of the letters was written by my mom to my dad when I was in high school, telling him she could not afford to buy me all the things that I needed and asking him if he would consider having me come live with him for a while. I was surprised she had written to him about this—we had never even discussed me living with my dad. This hurt my feelings; but it also made me realize how different my life, *and the lives of others*, might have been if I had moved from Florida, back to Ohio, when I was a teenager.

I returned to Phoenix right before the Christmas holiday and interviewed for another retail job at a clothing store in Paradise Valley mall. The store was based out of San Diego and carried beach, boating, and bar wear. I was hired as the assistant manager and would be starting in January. I was excited to finally be getting a chance to work with this type of clothing, beachwear. But I was now beginning to feel that I was getting too old to be cohabiting with my boyfriend, with no future plans for a family.

Wayne was a couple of years younger than me, and since he already had a son from his first marriage; he was not looking to have any more children. But I still saw a future with him. I had expressed my concerns on more than one occasion and told Wayne I didn't want to end up as some forty year old woman, shacked up with her boyfriend. I wanted to settle down; I was twenty-six now and wanted to think about starting a family before I reached the age of thirty.

My sister, Leigh, had been thirty when she had my nephew, Jordan, and I felt like I just didn't want to wait that long to have another child.

On New Year's Eve, we spent the beginning of the evening in a limo, barhopping with friends, and the rest of the evening at a party with some of Wayne's friends from the local bar. By the end of the night, I was half asleep on a couch at the house party we were attending, watching the pre-recorded Dick Clark celebration in New York.

Wayne came over and knelt down beside me—and proposed.

It turned out he had spent the entire evening showing everyone my engagement ring, but I had no idea he was proposing that night-at midnight!

I knew I had married my first husband too soon, and Wayne and I had a few things to sort out—children, religion, careers—so we put off setting a wedding date right away. I also had been on my own long enough that the decision was not going to be influenced by my parents. I wanted to make sure I'd known Wayne for at least a year and that we had discussed and agreed on our future plans before we got married. I was ready to settle down and start a family, but Wayne was not quite sure he wanted to do that again just yet.

It had been over 8 years since I had given birth to my baby girl, and I now felt more stable. I had a decent job in my field of work that I began in January, and I was engaged to a man that seemed to best fit me, and he had a good job also.

A few years earlier, when imagining the possibility of getting married a second time and settling down and starting a family, I thought 8/7/87 would be the perfect date for wedding—and a wonderful anniversary date. Now, it was actually happening—another opportunity for marriage and children. And it just so happened by the time August rolled around, Wayne and I would have been together for more than a year.

Who would have guessed that friends of ours, now living in Wayne's former apartment, would decide to get married on that exact same date? We had to find a new date for our wedding.

I didn't want to get married too close to a holiday, but when discussing dates, we soon realized our birthdays were just two weeks apart. The twelfth of the month would fall right in between them, and twelve had been my favorite number —since I was twelve years old! It was even a Saturday.

Within a couple months of working at my new job, I was promoted to manager when the current manager relocated to our new store in another mall, and the District manager asked me if I wanted to fill the new open position.

I was so excited, and I loved my job. I learned so much about being the manager of a beachwear clothing store.

Wayne and I had a simple wedding ceremony at the Courthouse, located in the shopping center next to our apartment complex, and we spent our honeymoon weekend at a nice resort in town. Because of our jobs, Wayne working Monday through Fridays and me working on Saturdays, we had to arrange our schedules and could only have a long weekend honeymoon at this time. We planned to take a week off the following year and spend it in San Diego.

Now, we were beginning our married life and looking for a house when, once again, I became unemployed. My district manager had decided to move back to Utah, and the new DM decided to lay off all of the current store managers and hire new ones. Our house hunting had to be put on hold.

I was beginning to understand the instability of working in retail, and I decided to look for a job in a different field.

I was hired to work in the home office of an insurance company where I would work Mondays through Fridays and have weekends off. It would be the first time in my life I wouldn't have to work full time every Saturday or Sunday.

Now we could afford a home—a starter home—and we found one close by that would allow Wayne to continue riding his bicycle to work. Wayne had been riding his bicycle to work from our apartment, and we didn't want to have to buy a second car.

We moved into our new house at the beginning of the New Year, and we spent the next year remodeling our modest home, which I found thoroughly enjoyable.

Both of our jobs were going well, and we loved working on our house and having friends over. I was hoping within the next year or so, we could start trying for a baby—I was ready to become a mom.

Even though Wayne's first child was being raised by his Ex wife, we made sure there was a room for him at our house too. Wayne's son rarely came to visit for more than a day at a time though. Wayne hadn't planned on having any more children, and I had always wanted two; so we *compromised* and decided one would be enough for us, for now. Though in theory, this would be my second child.

I hoped—and felt—that God would bless me with another daughter, a little girl for us to raise and share our lives with. I already had a nephew and a stepson, and I really wanted a baby girl that I could raise and dress up.

Now that I was actually *planning* for a baby, I had a long list of goals.

I not only wanted to have a girl, I wanted her to be born in the spring; the thought of being pregnant during a hot Phoenix summer was entirely unappealing. I even imagined she would be born in April, so she could have a diamond birthstone. I also decided to go off of birth control pills for three months, wanting to clear out my system of those toxins before I tried to get pregnant.

We were actually very careful, because I really wanted an April baby.

I estimated thirty-eight to forty weeks before April arrived to begin *trying* to conceive. We were going to start *trying* to get pregnant in July—I had delivered my first baby on her due date and assumed I could do so again.

Chapter 17

Southern California souvenir

1989

In the beginning of June, Wayne and I traveled to California to visit Leigh and Jordan. They were living on the beach, in Oceanside, California. Leigh and Rick had recently *divorced*. We planned a week long vacation, spending time on the beach, taking Jordan to the San Diego Zoo, visiting other relatives who were in town, and going out to restaurants and clubs in San Diego. Having such a great time being with my nephew, who was now four years old; we were excited about starting a family of our own. Our plan was to start *trying* to conceive once we returned home from our vacation.

We were back in Phoenix later in June and by July, we were back into our work routines, spending our free time with friends, going out to eat and to happy hours and parties. By the middle of the month, I realized I had not yet started my period since we had returned from California. This period was going to be the one that determined it was time to start *trying* to get pregnant.

It was a Saturday morning when I decided to take a home pregnancy test.

I was ecstatic when the test showed *positive*.

It seemed that the one and only time we'd failed to use birth control during our California trip, and totally unbeknownst to us, we had conceived. I couldn't help but recall my Mississippi doctors all reminding me "one time is all it takes." Of all people, I should have been the one to know better.

But this time, I was excited about the news!

That same day, my Mom and Edward flew in from Mississippi to visit us. They immediately asked if I was pregnant. Was I already glowing? My stomach had never really been flat again since I'd given birth to my first baby, so it was no surprise that when I was only about four weeks along, I already looked as though I was four months pregnant! Most people I knew didn't know about my first child—only family and good friends—so many thought I was pregnant with twins.

I started saving up vacation and sick time that I was accruing at work and added a couple of company paid quarterly bonuses to the pot as well. I planned on taking off twelve weeks for maternity leave. Our baby's due date was the 22nd of March, so I wasn't going to have my April baby unless he or she arrived late.

As the months went by, I was getting bigger and bigger by the day. My doctor sent me for an early ultrasound, wondering if perhaps I might be having twins, which of course, was still a thrilling idea to me.

The ultrasound confirmed I was only having one baby, and having known my date of conception; my due date remained as had been previously determined. But the weeks before the baby came were filled with stress.

One day I came home from the office to find Wayne home early from work and standing in the driveway. When I got out of the car and approached him, he told me that someone had broken into our house. Someone had gone through all of our personal things, including our baby's room. I felt so violated—and so unsafe. We had to install a home security system, which meant money was going to have to come out of our maternity leave savings.

And then, soon afterwards, my car started having one problem after another. Wayne finally told me it was time to get rid of it; he was concerned his pregnant wife would end up stranded on the side of the road on the way home from work. We took my car to a dealer we found through a friend and traded it in for a Ford Taurus, which was newer and had all sorts of upgrades, compared to my old Volvo. It was also more of a *family car*.

A couple of weeks after I got the new Taurus, I pulled into the bank parking lot, got out of the car and accidentally locked my keys and purse in it. The car had automatic locks, which I wasn't accustomed to; thankfully I still had my debit card on me.

I took twenty bucks out of the ATM and walked across the parking lot to a fast food restaurant and bought something to drink so I could get change for a phone call.

There was no answer at Wayne's place of work, which was a City utility yard, so I tried our neighbor's house. But they did not answer either—probably because it was before noon on a Saturday, and they rarely got up early on the weekends!

It seemed the only choice was to call a locksmith, but I didn't want to spend more money out of our maternity leave savings. I decided against the locksmith; and since Wayne's yard was in between the bank and our home, I decided to walk there. When I arrived, it was obvious that everyone working that day was out at a job site because the building was locked up tight. Now that I was halfway home, I decided I might as well just keep walking.

Once home, I was reminded that my house key was still in the car with my car key and my purse. I checked all the outside doors and windows of our house and, of course, they were all locked. By this time though, luckily, our neighbors were awake and answered the door, because I needed to use the restroom; so I ended up spending the rest of the afternoon with them. I waited there for Wayne to get home from work, hoping he wouldn't stop at the bar on the way home or work late. I just wanted to get my spare key out of our house and take it back to unlock my car door.

Luckily, he came right home from work that day.

Not too long after that, on another Saturday morning; I was about to pull into a parking spot at a grocery store, and the truck in front of me stopped and began to back up into the parking space. I honked my horn, but the driver didn't hear me and crashed into the front of my car. At the time, I was in my eighth month of my pregnancy. When the other driver saw how large my belly was, he was horrified and apologetic. He was driving a company truck and told me his employer's insurance would pay for any damages, and we exchanged information.

The following Monday, I contacted the company's insurance agent to file a claim and was told the owner of the company had informed his insurance company that I had run into his employee's truck, and the accident was my fault. Without witnesses or a police report, I couldn't prove otherwise. The repairs to my car meant more money would be coming out of our maternity leave savings.

In the midst of all of this, I was trying to keep myself calm; because I was certain stress would not be good for our baby. During my next ultrasound appointment, my doctor advised me that I had at least fourteen days or so until I would deliver. My baby had not turned or settled into the birth canal yet—my doctor also confirmed our baby was a girl.

Although our twenty-week ultrasound had revealed as much, Wayne wasn't going to be convinced until the baby arrived—this confirmation was exciting for me to hear. Three days later, while I was at work, nervously anticipating the delivery, I realized I should probably start carrying a towel or two in my car soon—in case my water broke while I was driving. I was on the phone that day with one of our Company's agents, when I told him I needed to disconnect. To my complete surprise, my water had broken. I walked quickly back to the restroom.

Some of my coworkers must have noticed my sense of urgency because when I came out of the bathroom stall, three people—including my manager and my two best work friends—were standing outside of it, asking me if I was okay. Their concern turned to excitement when I told them everything was okay as far as I knew, but my water had just broken!

I had been carpooling at that time with one of my friends'/coworkers', Shellie—who had been a good friend for a couple of years—Shellie drove me and my car back to my house. It was around eleven in the morning when we arrived. I called Wayne and told him to get home as fast as he could and then called the doctor's office to tell them what had happened.

"Are you sure?" they asked me.

"Yes, I'm sure!" I exclaimed.

They advised me to go to the hospital and told me my doctor was already there, delivering another baby. Wayne arrived at the house just a few minutes later, and after changing our clothes; we got back into the car, dropped Shellie off at home, and made it to the hospital by noon. I was taken immediately into the labor room. I told the nurse I was not feeling any contractions; they hooked me up to a monitor, and we began to watch the screen. According to *my* calculations, I was two weeks early.

I was hoping and praying everything was okay with our baby.

I had told the nurse I still couldn't feel a thing, but according to the monitor—and the nurse—I was indeed having contractions. Our daughter had just not settled into the birth canal, so she was not causing any pain—yet. Wayne sat there with me for a while, until the doctor came in and told the nurse that they were going to have to give me something to thin out my cervix. Our baby wanted out, and my body wasn't cooperating. The nurse said it was going to take a little while for the medicine to work and told Wayne if he wanted to, he could take a break.

Apparently, Wayne thought, *taking a break* meant leaving the building; he told me he was going to our neighborhood bar to tell everyone *we* were about to have our baby and would be back to the hospital shortly. I was a little concerned, but at that point, I couldn't do much about it.

I was just going to be laying in a hospital bed, waiting for something to happen.

The medication worked faster than anticipated, and it was about 1:30 pm when I began to feel the contractions. I asked for the phone and called the bar, (by now, I knew the number by heart); and when the bartender put Wayne on the line, I told him to leave immediately and come back to the hospital. My husband arrived within minutes and made up for his departure; he was back by my side, holding my hand and talking me through the contractions—even the nurses commented on his excellent coaching skills. When the doctor came back in to check on me, she asked if I wanted a *spinal block* for the pain. "No! I want to do this as naturally as possible!" If this was the last baby I was going to have, I wanted the full experience—something I had been denied with my first child.

"Let's get you into the delivery room then!" my doctor exclaimed.

Off we went. We arrived into the delivery room close to 2:45 pm, and Rachel arrived at 3:14 pm. They laid her on my chest, and I was in complete awe. It was impossible not to recall how I had missed out on this part of the birthing experience the first time around. I couldn't believe this was our baby!

My Doctor looked at us both and jokingly said, "The milkman?" Which was funny...but not!

Wayne and I were both blondes, but Rachel was born with darker skin and hair. Of course, we were surprised—we had expected our baby to have pale skin and light blonde hair, if she had any hair at all. But because she was born two weeks early, she was jaundiced, which caused yellowing of the skin and made her skin actually look darker. She had a small amount of dark brown hair and almond shaped, brown eyes, a German trait I've since learned is common on my side of the family.

Rachel was smaller than expected, only six pounds and fifteen ounces. Because of my size during pregnancy, all of us—even my doctor—expected a larger baby, at least eight pounds. The doctors and nurses told me because of her jaundice, I should not breast feed her. They were recommending a high iron formula, but I didn't totally agree with this approach. I didn't want to forgo breastfeeding, especially knowing how advantageous it would be, relative to the immune system. I'd grown up with asthma and allergies and hoped breast-feeding would help alleviate some of these possible problems for my daughter.

I missed dinner the day Rachel was born, but was able to enjoy a steak dinner the following evening before I was discharged, unfortunately alone, since Wayne didn't make it back to the hospital in time. We all left the hospital later that evening, after less than thirty-six hours.

During the first two weeks of her life, I gave Rachel the formula the hospital sent home with us, the majority of the time, and a little breast milk too; and she had to have daily blood tests to check her bilirubin levels. I also pumped breast milk, so I would be able to continue breast feeding Rachel full time once her levels were acceptable. After two weeks, I was able to breast feed her full time for the remainder of my maternity leave.

While I was on maternity leave, my brother, Edward, was getting married in Mississippi. I flew there with Rachel, and we spent a week with my mom and were able to attend all of the wedding functions for Edward and his soon to be wife. It made things so much easier, being able to breastfeed Rachel the entire time we were in Mississippi.

I was only able to stay home on maternity leave for a total of eleven weeks—though I had originally planned on staying home twelve weeks—but our finances were getting low, so I returned to work. Wayne took a week off work and stayed home with Rachel during her twelfth week, and then we found her a private daycare.

I continued breastfeeding in the mornings and evenings for a few months after I returned to work, wanting to breastfeed for at least six months. But Rachel weaned herself off of breast feeding when she realized that she could get much more to eat from the bottle of breastmilk or formula she was getting during the day.

We ended up trying several daycares, but none of them were a good fit. It turned out a woman I knew from the birthing classes we had taken—who had delivered her baby girl the same day as me—was a stay at home mom. She said she was willing to care for Rachel for us, and her rates were much more affordable than a daycare. She was a wonderful caregiver, and she kept daily notes for me.

This arrangement was ideal for about a year—until the caregiver started watching another child too. Rachel was the smallest of the three toddlers, and the other children overwhelmed her, making it more difficult to gain the attention of her caregiver. Her solution to getting what she wanted was to bite the other children to get her way. We had to find another sitter, but we weren't happy with any of the new daycares we found either. I really wished I could have stayed home with her over the course of the first two or three years, but it just wasn't possible.

When a new childcare center opened along my route to work, we decided to give it a try. Within a week, Rachel didn't want to leave—she loved her teachers and was learning new things every day

Chapter 18

The sunshine of our lives

1990's

Our daughter was the sunshine of our lives. Although we had a couple of reliable and affordable babysitters, we rarely went out without her—unless it was an *adults only* event or just *date* night.

I took Rachel on several trips throughout her early years; to Mississippi for Edward's wedding when she was a baby, to Michigan to visit my dad when she was only 18 months old, and to Ohio when she was three to visit him again before he passed away from cancer. I really wished he would have been alive to see her grow up—he would have been so proud of her. But I've always felt that he was watching over us from heaven. Rachel and I also traveled to Kentucky to visit friends and to Mississippi to visit family several times while she was still young. We often traveled without her dad.

Wayne and I did start taking Rachel on vacations to San Diego also when she was just two and that was always a family trip, which included Wayne, for years. Wayne was from California and a chance to go back to the beach was an easy decision for him to agree to.

On occasion, I picked up Rachel at daycare and took her with us to *Happy Hours.* As she got older, she loved winning stuffed animals from the crane vending machines located in several of the restaurants we frequented. Looking back, it may have been an irresponsible thing to do, but it certainly helped with her sociability skills. She would walk around the table, asking for dollars from our friends, so she could win more stuffed animals—and she rarely didn't get her way—all she had to do was smile.

When Rachel turned four, we took her to Disney Land and camped in our truck at their campground. We spent three days at the parks, and she had so much fun and fell in love with all of the Disney princesses.

Later that year, we took her with us camping with friends on the Colorado river—it was a nice long Memorial Day weekend vacation but not always a great place for kids to hang out. A young girl drowned that weekend and though we didn't know the family personally, we were heartbroken for them. We had to explain to our children what had happened, and it was a sad reminder of how fragile life could be.

Wayne had chosen to have a vasectomy when Rachel was just three months old, and I was scheduled to have a hysterectomy that summer, after she turned four years old. Now, she would definitely be our only child—though we had only planned on having one child.

I ended up having to take four weeks off work because of complications with my surgery, but I was able to spend a lot more time with Rachel that summer. My mom even came out to Arizona for a couple of weeks to help out. She was a little upset that we had chosen to have only one child, but I told her I had no choice; and Wayne had already taken care of that decision on his end years earlier. Edward and his wife would make up for Leigh and I only having one child each by having four children in the future! My mom still ended up having six grandchildren to love and pray for.

Rachel ended up staying at her childcare center through Kindergarten. When it was time to advance into the first grade, her Kindergarten teacher advised me that if I put her into a public school; she was going to be bored. She was already acing first grade level math and third grade level reading!

In the meantime, my Dad had left his three children some money and stocks, and I used some of my inheritance to put a downpayment on a new house. The neighborhood we had been living in since we bought our first house was not the nicest, and no further improvements to the property were worth doing there; because we knew we would never get our money back for them. I really wanted a pool and a decent neighborhood where Rachel could spend her time outside, playing.

Rachel was so excited about decorating her new, much larger, room with all the Disney princess'. We purchased a bunk bed for her room, with a double bed on the bottom for her and friends and a twin bed on the top for all of her stuffed animals!

We were also able to adopt our first pet—a small corgi mix puppy that would become Rachel's dog for the next ten years.

Soon, we began looking into private schools, and while they were cheaper than most of the daycares; the ongoing tuitions were going to be expensive for us. We found a Christian school close to our new home which was a little more affordable, When my mom found out we were enrolling Rachel in a Christian school, we were blessed in that she also offered to help pay the tuition there.

I remember taking Rachel to the school to take her *entrance exam*. She sat in a room, with just her future first grade teacher; and when they came out into the hallway to talk to us about her exam, her teacher told us that Rachel not only passed the exam but was going to be her class helper when school started.

"Rachel only missed one question on the exam, and it was the sequence of a snowman. I cannot even justify counting that question wrong, as she told me she has only seen snow once and has never built a snowman!"

Beginning with first grade, through sixth grade, Rachel made straight A's in all of her classes. She also represented her school in the district spelling bees during her first couple years of school. Rachel always did well in school; and for the most part, she liked all of her teachers.

When Rachel started going to a Christian school, we also decided to join a church that a couple of our friends attended. In addition to supporting Rachel in her Christian upbringing, there was also the thought that if the wives took the children to church, the husbands would follow. This didn't end up working out—especially not during football season—though they did attend Holiday services and any programs involving their children.

Wayne stopped going to church with us all together once his friends moved to another town.

As Rachel grew older, we signed her up for any and every extracurricular activity we could. Prior to elementary school, she had taken swimming lessons, ballet and tap classes, along with a few gymnastics classes.

When she entered the first grade, she wanted to take music lessons. She learned the basics of playing piano, flute and guitar. For several years, we also paid for her to take ice skating lessons. But ice skating was expensive in a city where snow rarely falls, and the sun shines the majority of the year.

Ice skating also got quite time consuming once Rachel reached competition level, and eventually she lost interest.

I took Rachel to all of these lessons and often the two of us would go out to eat or to see a movie or go shopping afterwards. Wayne was usually golfing or at the local bar with his friends. While he came to see her recitals, he rarely attended any of her lessons.

My mom would come out to Arizona from Mississippi quite often during the summers to visit Rachel and go to all of the lessons with us. It was great having her visit for a few weeks in the summers, so Rachel wouldn't have to spend the entire summer breaks in child care. My mom would also try to come out to Arizona to visit for a couple of weeks, starting right before the Christmas break, so she could attend any Holiday programs Rachel was in.

Wayne and I would also travel with Rachel and sometimes her friends to San Diego or other Southern California beach towns during the summers too. Rachel loved to ride on the carousel at Belmont Park, beginning at age two, and she still rides on it to this day! Like me, she also always loved the beach and probably always will.

I remember one summer my mom was visiting, and we were discussing the likelihood of my first daughter still living in Mississippi. I had given birth to her in Mississippi, and she had been adopted by a couple living in Mississippi; but people move.

We didn't realize it, but Rachel was listening to our conversation from a room nearby and came to me, crying, and asking why I had another daughter who didn't live with us. I was heartbroken. Rachel was only about eight years old at the time, and I had felt she was still too young to explain all of this to; but I had no choice now. I explained to her that I had had a baby when I was young, years before I knew her dad; and another couple, who could not have any children, was raising her. She wanted to know how old my other daughter was and who she was and where she lived. I told her that my first daughter was about 19 years old, but I didn't know who she was or where she lived. It was hard to explain how the private adoption had kept me from knowing her, but I felt that God had found the couple who became her parents. I did encourage her though by telling her that maybe God would bring her back into our lives one day, and she would get a chance to meet her.

Rachel thought it would be nice to have an older sister— since she only had an older half brother who she rarely saw —and he was a *boy*.

Chapter 19

Raising Rachel

2000

When Rachel was ten, we planned a cross country family trip to mark the *summer of 2000* and included Rachel's friend, Allie. We purchased a travel trailer; which we towed across Arizona and through New Mexico, Texas, and Louisiana. I remember us driving into New Orleans to spend a couple of nights and seeing all the families who lived in the small *shacks* we could see from the freeway. It was an eye opening experience for all of us, especially the girls, who had never seen this kind of poverty.

We continued to drive north through Mississippi and stopped in Brookhaven, so I could show them the Whitworth campus, where I had attended college. I was surprised it was still standing but saddened that it had a fence around it and a sign that stated the property had been given to the state and would become the Mississippi School of the Arts in the future. I hoped that the buildings would not all be destroyed—there was so much history there. I was happy to later learn that several buildings had been renovated, including the house I had stayed in as a pregnant teen and the dorm I had lived in while attending the college.

We drove up the Natchez Trace Parkway, and I pointed out milepost 127—where Anne and I had our car accident.

When we arrived at the Academy, we visited with my family still living there and dropped off the girls, so they could attend a summer camp program for a week.

Wayne and I camped at my mom's for a night and then drove back down through Mississippi to the gulf coast of Florida. We stayed a day in Pensacola and then drove across to the East coast of Florida to Saint Augustine and camped. We continued down the East coast to Daytona Beach then on to Fort Lauderdale, so I could show Wayne where I had lived during high school.

Since Wayne was from California, he was used to the dark sand beaches there and was surprised at how beautiful all the beaches were in Florida. We camped in the Fort Lauderdale area for a few days in hopes of meeting up with some of my old friends. I had hoped to introduce Wayne to friends of mine who still lived in the area, but I had lost touch with most of them. As it happened, June was the only person we were able to spend time with.

In preparation for our trip, I was looking up my old friends on the internet and found someone who told me I might be able to locate William through his biological father. It just so happened he lived in a nearby town to us, in Arizona—this surprised me!

During high school, I had mistakenly been under the impression that William's father was deceased; I found out later that his mother was widowed due to the death of his step father.

His biological father had moved, remarried, and was now living in Arizona with his wife and their two children.

I worked up the nerve to contact William's father to see if he could tell me where William was living. I had not heard from William since the summer of 1981. His Father claimed he did not have a current phone number or address for William. I wasn't sure if I should believe him, but I had no reason to think he would lie to me. As far as I knew, he didn't even really know who I was—maybe that was the problem. But he told me he would pass along a message and my information the next time he spoke to William.

When Wayne and I visited Fort Lauderdale, I also contacted William's brother, George, and asked him, too, if he would give my cell phone number to William. George gave me the impression it wasn't likely William would contact me, claiming William rarely contacted his own family, let alone *old girlfriends;* and I never did hear from William that summer.

We left Fort Lauderdale and drove to the Keys and camped in Key West for a few days, and then we headed north again towards Orlando.

Rachel and Allie flew to meet us there from Birmingham, Alabama; after Edward and his family drove them there from Northern Mississippi. We picked up the girls at the airport and spent five days and nights, camping at Disney World. We went to all of the parks, the girls rode as many rides as possible; and on the last day we were there, we hung out at their oldest water park.

It was a good thing it was our last day at the parks; as I broke my big toe, riding down the cement slide on an inner tube. I ended up riding all the way home with my foot up on the dashboard! That three week adventure was filled with special memories for all of us. And for the most part, everyone got along; and we had a great time!

The following year we returned to Florida, having flown to Mississippi first, instead of driving across the country. We rented a car in Jackson for this trip, and again delivered Rachel to the summer camp at the Academy. She planned on attending two weeks of camp this time, staying with my mom the weekend in between.

After leaving Northern Mississippi this time, Wayne and I drove back through Mississippi and Alabama to the gulf and headed south, down the West coast of Florida. We stayed a night in Fort Myers and visited Sanibel and Captiva Islands. We thought about driving over to Marco Island; but I was driving the car, and I couldn't convince myself to drive over a bridge, not knowing where it ended.

Instead, I drove south; and once we arrived in Naples, we decided to head to Fort Lauderdale again. I drove across *Alligator Alley,* a highway that cuts across the Southern Florida Everglades; and since I was driving this time, I ended up having to navigate the car through a heavy rain storm—with limited visibility—which was very stressful. We spent a few days in a hotel, centered between the two beach areas I had often frequented when I lived there. It was during this trip that I finally received a call from William. Wayne and I agreed to meet him and his girlfriend at a nearby bar that afternoon.

I had received William's call on our way back from the beach during an afternoon summer rain storm, and so we hurried to our hotel and dropped off our stuff and changed our clothes. We met William and his girlfriend in a dive bar he knew of, across the street from our hotel.

I remember wearing a sundress, with my hair still wet from the rain. I hadn't seen William for 20 years, and I surely wasn't looking my best; but I no longer really cared, I wasn't trying to impress anyone. I was happily married to my *surfer dude*, with an adorable, intelligent, and talented eleven year old daughter.

The four of us talked about our current lives and shared stories regarding the years since we had seen each other, over a couple of drinks.

William hadn't had any children of his own, but his girlfriend had children who it seemed as though he was very involved in helping raise. It didn't seem like the right time or place to discuss the daughter we'd given up years earlier for adoption.

Wayne knew he was meeting the father of my first daughter —I didn't know if William's girlfriend knew who I actually was or not. Our visit was cordial and when we left, William told me he would keep in touch; but I didn't hear from him again for several years.

Wayne and I continued our vacation and once again, we drove to Key West and stayed for a couple of days. On our way back through Florida, heading north to Mississippi, I drove on the turnpike through the entire state; and we made it back in record time.

We stayed a night in an awesome Bed & Breakfast near the Academy, picked up Rachel from camp the following day, and said our goodbyes to my family. Then we drove back down the Natchez Trace again to Jackson and flew back home to Arizona.

It would be our last Florida vacation for five years.

Back home, we returned to our normal routine. Rachel and I continued to attend church together and soon became more involved with church activities.

She and I had started watching the young children during some of the sermons, and I realized how great Rachel was with younger children—even at her young age of ten. At the end of 2000, I thought it would be good for me to start singing with our church's worship team. I was already singing with my former neighbors, during the *Open Mic* nights at our favorite pizza restaurant.

I had actually started singing a couple of years earlier with the band we hired for our annual parties, so I could sing a song to Wayne for our tenth anniversary party in September. The guitarist in the band had played for me, so I could sing a Jewel song for Wayne (but then I started wanting to sing at the *Open Mic* nights too). My former neighbor, Jim, and his wife and I all started performing together at the *Open Mic* nights—and sometimes we even had the nerve to sing *Heart* songs.

Often times Wayne would come to the restaurant where the *Open Mic* was held, so he could eat with Rachel and me and listen to me sing; and then he would leave and go down the street to the bar he patronized. He said he wasn't interested in listening to anyone else sing.

When I joined the worship team at our church, we practiced one night a week and led the worship music for one service on Sunday.

Then our church merged with another church, and we not only practiced one night a week but before the services on Saturdays and Sundays also, which became quite time consuming. All of this took time away from Wayne and Rachel, but they didn't seem to mind because they knew I loved to sing.

Rachel was involved with the Church youth group and even traveled to Mexico for a couple of summer mission trips and worked with the children there. I enjoyed telling my mom about Rachel's adventures in the mission field because, having done so much mission work herself, these stories made my mom immensely proud. I believe it was during one of these trips that Rachel realized she had a calling to go into the medical field—she wanted to work with sick children.

Wayne hadn't been much interested in Rachel's hobbies or other activities until she started playing softball in the fifth grade.

She was a pretty good short stop; but one day, in sixth grade, she got hit hard in her thigh with a ball and decided she didn't want to continue playing softball the next year. Rachel had also started playing basketball in fifth grade and it became her passion from fifth grade through her senior year.

Later, she also took up Volleyball and then joined the dive team the last two years of high school. Rachel seemed to do well at anything she tried to do.

Meanwhile, Wayne and I looked like a happy couple on the outside; involved in our daughter's school, attending her sporting events, and taking family vacations. One weekend though, things would all change.

One Saturday, I was sitting at the desk on the first floor of our house, paying all our bills online. Wayne looked down over the railing from the second floor and said he was tired of all of *his* money going to pay bills. "We're going to file for bankruptcy," he declared.

I thought he was joking, but I was shocked when he told me he was serious. We were able to pay all our bills—there were just a lot of them—because we went out a lot, and we took a lot of vacations! But he didn't stop with that—he told me that after we filed bankruptcy, he was going to file for a divorce!

I couldn't believe it! We had spent so many years taking vacations and having birthday-anniversary parties. We had built our new house and remodeled it just like we wanted it and thought we had good equity in it for the future. We had even talked about our future plans, when Rachel would be going off to College and Wayne would be able to retire from his job with the City.

He never seemed to worry about the bills when we were doing something he enjoyed doing.

He asked me for a divorce in January, the following year after we returned from our two week vacation in Florida— the year we were going to be celebrating our fifteenth wedding anniversary. We spent most of that year unhappily cohabiting, trying our best to get along and parent our twelve-year old daughter, all the while with the strain of a bankruptcy and the possibility of a divorce hanging over our heads.

Rachel continued to attend her private Christian school; and that summer flew back to Mississippi, by herself, to attend camp for a couple of weeks, one last summer.

Wayne and I continued working on renovating our house, and everything continued to look fine—from the outside.

We had met with a bankruptcy lawyer that Wayne contacted and ended up filing bankruptcy on some of our credit accounts, which eased a little of the strain.

I did not encourage Wayne to file for a divorce and told him if that was really what he wanted, he was going to have to make the first move and file the papers, because I would not. I also told him I would not withdraw Rachel from her school, nor was I willing to sell our house. I encouraged him to think more about his decisions when he was sober.

Later that year, Wayne's father became very ill and passed away soon afterwards. Though they had never been really close, losing his father had a big impact on him; and for a short time, his attitude changed.

Through all of this, Rachel survived our strained home life; but when she received her first "B" in seventh grade, we worried she may have to curtail some of her activities. While we wanted her to be a well-rounded child, we did not want her sports or friendships interfering with her studies.

But after some discussion, we determined a couple of B's would be acceptable—for now—and she continued participating in her many extracurricular activities.

In ninth grade, Rachel transferred to the public high school near our house, after being accepted into their International Baccalaureate program. This would ultimately benefit all of us by giving her a chance to earn a full college scholarship to an Arizona State college.

She also became her school's basketball team's MVP her Freshman year.

Even in all her advanced studies, Rachel still received high marks in her classes. But when she developed more of an interest in boys, the impact to her grades was apparent.

Rachel met her first boyfriend, Eddie, at the age of fourteen, when she attended a party with her best friends in Fountain Hills. She was fifteen when they started dating, officially, and they remained together for almost a year. Rachel didn't discuss with us what brought about the break-up, but they did remain friends. I think a lot of the original problems stemmed from the strain of the parents having to give them rides to see each other, and they lived twenty-five miles apart. Needless to say, Rachel had spent a lot of time that year at her best friends' house—in order to see Eddie too.

Rachel and I did not actually sit down and discuss boys and sex, but I did tell her I was always available for questions and gave her lots of information to read and consider— which she was comfortable in doing.

I also explained to her more about the circumstances that lead to me having a baby at age eighteen, so she would realize the seriousness of a casual physical relationship with a boy. She was an intelligent and level headed young lady, and I knew most of the friends she hung out with and their parents too, so I wasn't too concerned.

In 2006, when Rachel was sixteen, and with her best friend, Maye tagging along; we returned to Florida to vacation.

Maye had become Rachel's best friend when Rachel started hanging out with her older sister in Elementary school and spending more time with the two of them in Fountain Hills.

Maye went on several vacations with us to San Diego and Fort Lauderdale. Actually, over the years, we had taken many of Rachel's friends to San Diego, and she tried to teach each of them how to surf.

Wayne and I had talked about investing in a rental property while we were in Florida this time, and so we checked out a few condominiums in the Fort Lauderdale beach area.

We stayed in a Marriott timeshare resort during our first week, thanks to Maye's parents. We rented a private condo during our second week; but after some consideration, we decided to purchase a timeshare in the Marriott resort.

It had been several years since Wayne mentioned filing for a divorce, and things seemed to be back to normal—though never quite back to the way they used to be between us.

Rachel had made another good friend, named Tina, at the high school she attended. Tina was the friend she hung around with, mostly during the week, because she was also in the IB program at their school. All of the girls became good friends and they would hang out together, in Phoenix and in Fountain Hills, quite often.

Rachel's girlfriend's moms became *second moms* to Rachel and she traveled often with their families too. Her friends' families loved to go boating and snow boarding and Rachel enjoyed both of these activities.

When we returned home from Florida that summer, Rachel began her junior year of high school. She also started dating a young man, named Adrian, from our church in Scottsdale. Adrian usually came to Rachel's basketball games to watch her play and many times he would take her and Tina out to eat afterwards or they would all go to see a movie.

During this time, my sister, Leigh, had been living in her own apartment in Phoenix, working part-time and collecting disability. Years earlier, she had been diagnosed as being bi-polar and was unable to work full time. My nephew, Jordan, had moved back to Northern California, when he was still young and lived with his Dad until he went away to college in Southern California.

One afternoon, Leigh was found unconscious in her apartment by a friend, and I was called at work to go to a nearby hospital emergency department. I spent the evening with her, holding her hand, and also sat in the emergency waiting room, contacting family. The doctors could not tell me what had happened to her—only that she was found on her bathroom floor, unconscious and covered in bruises. The hospital was running tests to see if she had overdosed on something, but so far had found no illegal drugs in her system.

After several hours, I was told I should go home, and they would contact me with any news.

In the meantime, Jordan drove over from College in Southern California with a friend and stayed with us for a few days to be with his mom.

It was later discovered that Leigh had actually overdosed on over the counter pain medicines. The doctors told us that Leigh had no brain activity; and if she did survive, she would be in a vegetative state.

Leigh had a *do not resuscitate* order on file with her best friend, and so we had to make the decision a couple of days after she was admitted to the hospital to take her off of life support.

Her family and friends were holding hands, surrounding her bed, when the life support was turned off—it would be the first time I saw anyone die—and not just anyone, but my one and only sister.

Rachel and Adrian helped make a collage of old pictures for Leigh's memorial service at our church. Many of her friends at that time did not know much about her past. Few of them had even seen pictures of Leigh when she was younger, and several of them didn't know she had been a model for over ten years or that she had been married twice before she met Jordan's Dad.

Along with our Pastor, Jordan spoke at his mom's memorial service.

It was so touching to see how mature he was through all of this and how well he handled the situation.

I had been storing some of Leigh's belongings in our garage and had the task of cleaning out her apartment also and going through her things to decide what should given to Jordan. We also needed to decide what we could donate, sell, give to friends, or wanted to keep in the family. My sister (and Jordan when he was younger) had collected many things that they hoped would possibly be worth money in the future; but we had no use for many of the items at this time and so donated them to charity or gave them to family or friends.

A few months later, Jordan graduated, summa cum laude, from Pepperdine University. Wayne, Rachel, Tina, and I drove to Southern California to attend his graduation; we met up with Rick and his current wife and their daughter and spent some time with them also.

Rachel and her second boyfriend, Adrian, did not date long but remained friends until they began their senior years at different high schools, and Rachel stopped attending our church on a regular basis.

During Rachel's senior year, she met another young man, Marc, through her friends who lived in Fountain Hills. They started dating later that year and continued dating through the summer and when Rachel began attending college in Tempe the next fall.

I had hoped Rachel would continue wanting to play basketball in college; but once she started dating this young man, she told me she was tired of dressing in shorts and T-shirts, tired of practicing, and wanted to take a break from sports.

Marc's family owned their own company and were very successful. They often held parties for the kids, and they traveled to their cabin near an Arizona ski resort in the Winters. Since Rachel had learned to surf during our California vacations when she was young, snowboarding had been an easy transition for her.

Rachel and her new boyfriend's relationship got off to a good start, but once she went to college and began living on campus in Tempe, things became strained. I noticed many similarities between Marc and my first husband, Ethan. Marc, too, seemed plagued with insecurities; and jealousy became a big problem in their relationship.

I did not want Rachel to end up in a relationship like the one I had during my first marriage, but I could not tell her what she could or couldn't do when it came to romance.

I was not going to repeat the same mistakes my mother had made with me. Instead, I tried, when appropriate, to gently express my opinions.

In time, she would come to realize what she really wanted in a life partner.

Chapter 20

Deja Vu

2009

During the spring of Rachel's first year of college, Wayne and I took Rachel, Maye and Tina to Fort Lauderdale for a vacation and to celebrate Rachel's nineteenth birthday. Now that we owned a timeshare, this had become an annual vacation for us for several years. We had fun, celebrating Rachel's birthday and being a part of the spring break crowd in Fort Lauderdale. Rachel, Maye, and Tina were often the cutest girls on the beach, so we kept an eye on them and accompanied them almost everywhere they went —most of the time.

We returned home on a Saturday, took the girls out to dinner; and then they headed to Fountain Hills for the night, before Rachel and Tina drove back to their dorm in Tempe on Sunday.

But by Sunday evening, the atmosphere in our house had taken a turn for the worse.

I wasn't expecting what happened that evening at all, but early Sunday evening, Wayne and I were watching television; Wayne had spent most of his afternoon at the local bar, and I had spent most of mine, still unpacking and finishing laundry—and He told me we needed to talk.

He said he *wanted out.*

"What are you talking about?" I said.

He'd consumed a few beers that afternoon, and I was assuming he'd just had a few too many.

He said he wanted out of our house—and our marriage.

His decision seemed to all be based on our finances...

We had borrowed against the equity in our house to pay off some more of our debts, and now the country was in the middle of a major housing market crash. We had recently learned that our house was worth half of what we owed the bank for it and the equity credit line. This was something he blamed on me; it had been my suggestion to refinance the house and take out the credit line to pay off our cars and other credit, the credit cards having financed our vacations since our bankruptcy years earlier. And paying all our bills, was my job, after all.

How was I to know the entire housing market was about to implode, and our property would drop so far in value?

But I didn't believe this was Wayne's real reason for wanting a divorce; instead, I think it had become an excuse. We'd already been down this road the first time he told me he wanted a divorce.

I wasn't about to spend another year like I had that previous year—adding to his now obvious disinterest in spending time with me, and me always wondering where he was and who he was with. So, I decided to call his bluff. "Fine, if you want out so badly, the first thing you can do is move out of our bedroom and into the guest room—downstairs!"

I thought perhaps this might sober him up a little to the reality of what he was suggesting. To my surprise, he went upstairs and moved all of his personal belongings to the guest bedroom on the first floor. But he'd spent time living in the guest room before, shortly after he'd asked me for a divorce the first time—over seven years earlier. I really didn't think he would follow through with a divorce and assumed it was just going to be another rough patch in our now twenty-one plus year marriage.

But every day we grew further and further apart.

Later, when I began to question him about his many absences from home, he claimed he was seeing a counselor, who had referred him to a psychiatrist; and he was going to appointments at the end of most workdays. Previously, he had attended AA meetings, in an attempt to *better himself* when we separated the first time.

Of course, I later found out that as far as the *doctor appointments* went, he'd only seen each of the doctors once.

Apparently, the bartender and Wayne's friends (none of them really my friends) at his neighborhood hangout, were the ones providing his therapy, along with *Bud*. While he sat at the bar, bemoaning his fate; I would pick up an iced green tea from Starbucks and spend my evenings, eating alone, reading or watching television. During the work week, Wayne would be in his room by 7 pm, either already asleep or watching television.

Wayne switched his schedule and began working Wednesdays-Sundays, and I was still working Mondays-Fridays, so we rarely ran into each other.

At one point, I started going out, attending *Open Mic* nights at various places during the week and going to my friends' music gigs. On the weekends, I began staying out later and later.

I was tired and bored with my solitary routine of eating dinner alone, reading a book or just sitting at home, in front of the television—especially once it was summer and everything on TV was in reruns!

In the midst of all of this, Rachel had been hired to work for my employer during the summer months, as soon as her classes ended. She had previously worked two, ten hour days with me when she had lived at home. Now she would drive to the office from her apartment and work a few days each week.

We would try to talk during our breaks, but she was having difficulty understanding what had happened between her dad and me.

When she questioned him, he claimed to have *screwed up* and wanted to fix things; but said I wasn't willing to do so, because I had starting seeing someone else. I explained to her that while I had been going out, spending more time with friends, that I was absolutely not dating anyone and doing so was the last thing on my mind at that time. I informed her that we had unofficially separated back in March, when she had returned to college after our vacation. "We first tried to work things out by attending our church's couple's class, but that just seemed to make things worse; and your dad refused to go to marriage counseling." I told her. I explained to Rachel that I really didn't think her dad was being honest with her about our breakup. He would apologize to me via text when he was sober, and then he would send me nasty messages when he was drinking. Yet, he rarely ever spoke to me when he was at home. It was clear to me that even though he thought he still loved me, he didn't want to be married to me any longer. I made it clear to Rachel that Wayne's claim that I was dating someone else was not the cause of our break-up. It was much more complicated than that, but he refused to take responsibility for his role in any of it.

I also revealed to her that the situation was most likely permanent.

236

I couldn't handle the stress any longer and had to accept that our marriage was over. I prayed for Wayne, and I prayed about our marriage; but without some major changes in our situation and a commitment from Wayne, I couldn't see our marriage continuing. I had tried what I knew to do to repair our marriage and though I was still making mistakes, I couldn't change Wayne's ways. All I could do now was make the best of the situation, try to maintain peace between us, and move on.

Sometime after Wayne and I had agreed to divorce, I spent a few days hanging out at the Marriott resort near our house. Hanging out by our pool at our house was not an option at this point, and weekends by the pool at the resort were one of the perks when owning a Marriott timeshare. I was hoping to hold on to our timeshare, since we were planning on selling our house at some point in the future. I figured I would get use out of it locally and hopefully continue visiting the resort in Fort Lauderdale in the future.

Rachel came to stay with me overnight, since school was over now, and we spent most of the day out by the pool and then went out to eat dinner at one of the restaurants nearby. The next morning, the phone awoke us at 7 am—it was my friend, Rich, calling from Florida. He had forgotten there was a three hour time difference this time of year between Florida and Arizona.

I think Rachel was suspicious; but I explained to her that he was just an old friend of mine, and we had recently reconnected on Facebook. He had an interest in renting my week that year at our resort in Florida, and I had told him I would be at the resort in Phoenix for the weekend; but I didn't think he would call me there.

I hadn't seen Rich since I spent the summer in Fort Lauderdale in 1981, when I was in College; but we'd gone out a couple of times, and I had fond memories of him. We'd actually been friends since we met at church, in the Youth group, when we were teenagers. We ended up talking on the phone several times while Wayne and I were separated and planning on filing for a divorce, and it was nice to have someone to talk to—along with a male perspective on things. He had been through a similar situation in the past.

In the meantime, Wayne had been looking for an apartment located between our house and his work, so he could still ride his bicycle to the yard. He had purchased an old truck he drove around when it was raining or too cold to ride his bicycle, but that was rare in Phoenix. By the beginning of the summer, he had found a small apartment he felt he could afford, about a mile away from our house, on his route to work. He signed a lease to start in August because he wanted to save more money, and so he planned on living in our house until the end of July.

In June, I had been invited to attend an *Open Mic* at another restaurant, by the person hosting the *Open Mic*. It was on a Tuesday night, at a small English Pub down the street from our house. A few of my friends from the O*pen Mic* at our favorite pizza restaurant had also been invited, and so I thought I'd get out of the house for the evening and meet up with them.

When I arrived at the Pub, I didn't see anyone else I knew there, except for the *Open Mic* host; and so I sat in an empty seat at the end of the bar. There was an empty seat next to me, in between me and another man; who was also sitting alone, at the end of the bar. When I sat down, he said, "Hi," and introduced himself to me as Alan. He asked me if I was there for the O*pen Mic*. I said, "Hi," introduced myself and told him I had been invited by a friend and was just there to listen. I got out my book (I always brought a book when I went to *Open* M*ic* nights—to read during the breaks), ordered a light beer, and began to read. Alan started talking to me and asking me if I had ever been to this *Open Mic* before, and if I knew anyone performing. I told him I only knew the host, and I usually attended *Open Mic* nights at other locations. I also shared with him that I used to perform, but I was without a guitarist at the time. He told me he played guitar, mostly electric; but was thinking of practicing his acoustic guitar playing more, possibly at an *Open Mic*.

He also told me that he lived close by and had just stopped by for a beer after work and to see what this *Open Mic* stuff was all about.

I shared with Alan about some of the other *Open Mic* locations I attended in the area and told him that he should check them out too.

I put my book away when the first performer started, realizing I probably was not going to be reading much since I had found someone to talk to during the breaks.

Alan told me that he had a full-time job as an audio/video engineer at a company in Scottsdale—which was owned by an older female he had worked with for approximately 20 years. He was now the only employee and was in charge of all the projects his boss was hired to complete. He was also an electric guitarist who played in a couple of bands, one locally and one in Prescott. He said he often traveled out of town for gigs and had just returned from Prescott, where he played the previous weekend with one of his bands and also celebrated his birthday.

It was obvious from our conversation that his talent level was much better than most of the people we were hearing that evening. We talked throughout most of the evening, and he was a very nice man. He actually looked at me (with his striking blue eyes) and listened to me during our entire conversation.

He asked me if I was married, and I told him I was currently separated; but my soon to be Ex husband was still living in our house, and sometimes I just needed to get out of the house. He told me he was recently divorced and had the same problem before he had moved out. His Ex wife still lived in their condo.

We closed down the bar (at 9 pm), and he walked me to my car and hugged me goodnight. He told me that it was great meeting me and talking to me, and he hoped to see me again.

Wayne was asleep when I arrived home, and I realized that I was in a very strange place in my life.

Alan and I began running into each other at the various other *Open Mic* nights I had told him about, and we sat together and talked. During the course of our discussions, I explained my situation; I wanted to make sure he knew I wasn't interested in dating, let alone ready for anything serious, as I was still legally married to Wayne. As it turned out, Alan was on the same page; since he was newly divorced himself. As far as I was concerned, I was just happy to have made a new friend, and one that loved music.

Wayne had agreed to pay half the mortgage until we sold our house, and I agreed to live in it and take care of it; providing he would help me once a week with the pool and the yard.

He didn't think I would be able to keep up my half of the house payment and pay all the utilities, but I told him I was advertising for roommates. I was not going to just walk away from the house we had built together and put so much work into.

I made arrangements with two female college students to rent the empty upstairs bedrooms, and they were scheduled to start moving in the first weekend of August. This would give me about a week to clean and touch up paint in the rooms after Wayne moved out. I had planned on moving all of Rachel's belongings from her large room upstairs, into the guest room downstairs, after Wayne moved out; and I had cleaned the carpet in the bedroom.

After Alan and I knew each other for about six weeks and had run into each other at several *Open Mic* nights, he invited me to come to see him play at one of his shows— with the band he played in, locally.

It was late in July and very hot, and I got dressed up in a new sundress I'd purchased during our last trip to Florida that spring. I thought I was in the house alone the entire time I was getting ready; but when I turned out the upstairs lights and began walking down the stairway in the dark, the corner living room light suddenly clicked on and Wayne was sitting in my recliner. He had parked outside and let himself in through the front door, instead of the garage door; so I wouldn't hear him.

He asked where I was going, and I told him I was going out with some friends to listen to a band. He made some crude remark about the way I was dressed; I told him it was July, it was hot; and I wasn't going to sit at home and spend my weekend watching television.

I also reminded him that he was already divorcing me and would be moving out within days, so he really couldn't tell me what to do or who I could spend my time with. I left, with Wayne still sitting in the house—I hoped.

I didn't have far to go to get to the gig, but I took the longest route possible, unnecessarily driving through several neighborhoods; so I could be certain I wasn't being followed. The last thing I needed was for my soon to be Ex husband making a scene in a strange place in front of my *new friends*.

The venue was a small dive bar and grill—and it was packed. I found a place to park but hesitated getting out of my car—did I even want to go in? I wondered if Alan would remember inviting me...

Did he expect me to show up?

I mustered up the courage and locked up my car and headed toward the front door. When I entered the bar, I glanced around to surmise the scene and let my eyes adjust.

I looked towards the *stage* and within a minute, Alan was escorting me to a seat at a table right in front, adjacent to the dance floor. He introduced me to the other people at the table—friends of the band members. He excused himself and came back shortly with two light beers in hand. I struck up a conversation with Carly, who I learned was the band's part-time manager and attended many of their gigs. I told her this was my first time hearing the band, and that I usually hung out at *Open Mics* or acoustic gigs. Carly promised me they were good, and that I was going to love listening to them.

The band began to play, and I did my best to watch all of the players, trying not to be too obvious that I was actually checking out Alan. (Many of the electric guitar players I had met over the years seemed to be a little conceited and not as good as they thought they were.) I was waiting to see if Alan was as talented as I was now assuming he was.

Marie, the lead singer, was the only girl in the group, and while small of stature, she had a big, strong voice. The drummer and bass guitar player were talented as well, and everyone in the band sang vocals. I had not seen this much talent in many of the local bands I had run across since I had been in Arizona, although there had been one I had followed around years earlier with a friend of mine from work.

I found out later that one of Alan's bands used to often play at the same clubs with that band, but that was in the early 80's, before I moved to Arizona. So, most likely, I had never seen any of Alan's previous bands; so I had never seen him play guitar.

As it turned out, Alan was not just a good guitarist, he was an amazing guitarist—and he sang too! I agreed with Carly —the band was great. I spent much of the night on the dance floor with Carly, as we seemed to be the only two girls without dates that wanted to dance.

When the band was done for the night, it was quite late. I wasn't looking forward to going home to a dark house or possibly running into Wayne again, so I offered to help pack up the equipment. I knew very little about packing up equipment—as the only things I had to pack up in our church worship team were the microphone cords. Everyone was patient and kind, showing me just what to do; and I got to talk more to all of the band members. They were all talking about going out to breakfast and invited me to come along. I hadn't had dinner, and I was quite hungry. It sounded like fun.

Alan and I arrived at Denny's in our cars first, and we got a table by the window. Alan needed to keep an eye on his car and his equipment.

Soon we realized the other band members were not joining us; it seemed they had decided we wanted to be alone, although that had not been my intention. The two of us ordered food; and we spent the next couple of hours, drinking coffee and getting to know each other better.

When we finally went outside to leave, we stood by my car and continued our conversation.

It was now after 4 am, and I really didn't want to go home and run into Wayne; who would be heading out the door shortly to go to work. "Maybe I should wait until he leaves for work," I said, "or maybe I could somehow sneak back into the house, through the front door." It had worked for Wayne earlier; I could just park outside.

At any rate, it was time for me to go home.

As I got ready to leave, Alan hugged me goodbye, like he always had—and then he pulled me tight and kissed me. I was completely taken aback. This was the first time he had done anything other than hug me during a hello or goodbye. I was shocked! I asked him why he kissed me—what had changed? He said he had decided he really liked me, but he reassured me that he understood my situation entirely; and he knew I wasn't ready to get involved again—yet.

It was nice to know he cared enough about me to let his guard down, but I knew he wasn't ready to get involved again either—and certainly not with someone who was *technically* still married. I went home and went to bed, somehow having avoided Wayne's departure. I was certain he was angry with me for having not come home the night before, but I didn't care. I had to accept that Wayne and I were finished a long time ago.

As our divorce had become more and more of a reality, I had been pondering the possibility of returning to live in Florida. Now the thought came to mind that perhaps I didn't want to move away from Arizona. It was the first time in months that I had gone to bed feeling happy.

Wayne was scheduled to move out of the house on the last Friday of the month, but when I came home early from work the previous day; I was surprised to find him in the house, his truck parked in the backyard—moving his things out through the back French doors. When I asked him why he was moving a day early, he told me that he had stopped by the apartment complex on his way home from work, and they had given him the keys already; so he had just decided not to wait.

I couldn't help but remember my first husband, Ethan, moving out of our apartment while I was still at work...

I wondered how I would have felt if I would've come home at my usual time and only found a half empty house and a note from Wayne—if even that.

I assumed this decision had been made recently when he didn't hear me come home at night before he went to sleep; but I wondered aloud where my daughter was, as she had volunteered to come home with her truck to help him move. Wayne told me that he had told Rachel not to bother to come to the house to help him move, he could do it himself; but instead asked if she would come to his apartment the next day, after work, to help him get organized. I was hurt by this bit of news; she wasn't speaking to me much by this time, still blaming me for the break up—and now an opportunity for me to see and talk to her had been lost.

As Wayne was packing up his things, he told me to decide what furniture he could take, and what I wanted to keep. We had already decided this, but as usual, he wasn't really listening. He took enough to furnish his apartment, including the bedroom furniture in the guest room. I had already planned to move Rachel's old bedroom furniture into the downstairs guest room, so she would have her own place to stay when she came home from college. I would only be alone for a little over a week before my roommates started moving in, and I had a lot to do; so I was actually glad Wayne decided to go ahead and move out a day early.

This would give me the entire weekend to clean and paint and move things; and I had already taken the following day off work, so now I could get started cleaning and painting and moving furniture early.

I was up all night, working on cleaning the guest room—which had not been cleaned in months.

Sadly though, Rachel never did come home to visit me that summer. After school was over, we had helped her and her now college roommate, Tina, move out of the dorm and into a new apartment in Tempe. Most of the time, the two of them were either with their friends or boyfriends in Fountain Hills when they weren't working. Rachel did visit her dad a few times; but she never spent the night at our house the rest of that year—even though we had reconnected finally.

By the beginning of the school year, actually closer to my birthday in September; I drove to Tempe one day after work to see her apartment—and meet her new puppy!

As this puppy grew, it became obvious that it wasn't going to be staying in her apartment much longer; I was going to be acquiring another dog, along with our family dog that came with the house and my roommate's dog that had moved in with her.

Chapter 21

Music again comforts me

When Wayne moved out, it had already been almost five months since he had moved downstairs; and we began living separate lives. Now that we were living apart, we scheduled a meeting with a mediator to set a date for the divorce filing. It just so happened that the available date fell on my birthday, in September.

Alan and I had started spending more time together, and I could not believe how well we got along. He was such a caring and thoughtful man, always wanting to know my opinion on what I wanted to do at night, where I wanted to go eat dinner (or he would cook for us), and what I wanted to watch on television. We talked about everything— I had never experienced this level of communication with a man.

I started to realize though that I wasn't getting enough sleep. I was working four, ten-hour days, getting up at 4:30 am to get ready for work, but staying up late every night with Alan, watching television, laughing, and talking. I told Alan that I needed to start leaving his place by 10 pm, so I could get at least six hours of sleep each night before work. This lasted for a short time, until one evening, when he was off at band practice and I was at his apartment, watching television, waiting for him to come home—and I fell asleep on his couch.

After that, we determined if I just stayed at his place—at least when I didn't have to go to work the next day—I could still get six to eight hours of sleep without having to drive back to my house late at night. Those nights we stayed up, watching the late shows, I would just sleep at Alan's place. It may be hard to believe, but it's true; we were just sleeping. We were thoroughly enjoying our time together and just getting to know one another better. Alan could talk to you about almost anything—he was very intelligent and easy to carry on a conversation with. Neither one of us was ready to rush into another physical relationship—at least I wasn't, since I was still *legally* married to Wayne.

My oldest roommate, Valerie, was in her early twenties and had gone back to school to finish a dual degree. She loved music and played guitar and piano, sang and wrote songs, danced and worked out at the gym also. She also rode a motorcycle. Valerie worked full time—all while going to school full time and making straight A's. She was amazing and loved hanging out with Alan and me whenever she got a night off work. She was renting Rachel's old room; it was bigger than the upstairs guest room/office, and she was willing to pay more per month to store all of her things at the house.

My younger roommate, Carey, moved into the smaller guest room/office upstairs. This was the first time Carey had lived on her own, as she was just starting college.

She spent a lot of time hanging out with friends and just watching television in her room—she didn't really talk much to us, except to let us know if she wasn't going to be back to the house at night, so I didn't worry. Carey would drive to her parent's house, in a nearby town, most weekends, with her dirty laundry—and return with clean clothes and sheets and towels and food for the week. I had a feeling she wasn't going to stay for the six-month minimum I had required on the lease; so I told her as long as she gave me a thirty-day notice, she could leave any time.

Soon after my roommates moved in with me, my air conditioner broke down. Being as it was still summer in Arizona, it was not an optimal situation. I told the girls they were welcomed to stay at the house and just run all of the fans, or they could stay with friends for the night. I apologized and told them I would have the A/C repaired as soon as possible—hopefully the next day.

I didn't really have all the money to get it fixed, and so I asked Wayne to pay for half of the repairs, since we still jointly owned the house. I ended up staying over at Alan's place and luckily was able to schedule the repair service for the next day.

Wayne told me he couldn't give me any more money until the following Friday, after he got paid; it was Alan who offered to help me pay for the repairs.

Since Rich had decided not to rent my timeshare week that year, and I was still able to use it; I decided to transfer my week in Florida to the resort near my house and have a *staycation* in September for my birthday. I had already requested time off from work, a year in advance, for the entire holiday week and had originally planned to celebrate my forty-ninth birthday at the resort in Florida.

I hung out by the pool, in the sun, for a few days and thought a lot about my future; and if I wanted to stay in Arizona or move back to Florida.

I came to the realization that I wasn't quite fifty years old yet and had already been married twice, divorced once and was currently separated with a second divorce in the works soon. To add to that, I also had one daughter who was currently not speaking to me much and one daughter who I still had no idea where she was, what she was doing, or even who she was.

On the positive side, I'd lost nearly twenty pounds since my separation and was once again wearing a bikini by the pool, though I still had a small *baby belly*. Perhaps this would be the last year I could get away with wearing a bikini by the pool. I assumed I had grandchildren out in the world somewhere and the thought of me being a fifty year old grandmother, in a bikini, by the pool, made me wonder…*when are my bikini days actually going to end?*

I invited Alan to come and join me at the resort for the Holiday weekend and was looking forward to spending more time with him, hanging out in the shade by the pool. He was not a sun worshipper, but it didn't seem to matter as much to me now; since I really didn't feel the need to hang out in the sun nearly as much as when I was younger.

While I was on my *staycation*, Wayne contacted me, so that we could meet; and he could give me his share of the money for the repairs to the air conditioner. I explained to him that I was at the resort for my birthday week, and asked him if he could bring the money to me there. When he arrived outside the lobby to meet me, he behaved as though I didn't deserve *his* money. He told me that since I was now (obviously) dating someone, they should be responsible for household repairs. Not only was I angry by his suggestion, I was appalled. I had no idea how he even knew I was seeing anyone—unless he had been spying on me from afar. I made it clear the house was no one's responsibility but ours. Why would he think that someone I was dating—who didn't even live in the house—would be responsible for repairs to a house they had no ownership in?

Now that Wayne knew I had met someone, he told me we better file for divorce soon; he didn't want me *cheating* on him. At this point, I was pretty certain Wayne was the one who had been *cheating*, not me. But I had no proof and didn't really care.

254

I realized his intent was to make me look like the *bad guy* in all of this. I told him I would see him at the mediator's office Tuesday to get the divorce paperwork started.

I still had an awesome holiday/birthday weekend with Alan and then spent Tuesday, running errands and signing paperwork at the mediator's office with Wayne-while Alan returned to work.

Wayne and I discussed the terms of our divorce with our mediator, and she helped us determine what each of us would take from the marriage. The mediator told me I was entitled to part of Wayne's retirement fund/pension. Although we had used part of my retirement savings to fund Rachel's first year of college, I told the mediator I didn't want any of his retirement. I did, however, make it known that I wanted the Marriott timeshare in Florida. Wayne had never really used the resort except to travel with us as a family, and I had always been the one to reserve our trips to Florida. If it was left to me, I would continue using it. If he took sole possession of it, he would probably just sell it for a discounted price and keep the money.

He told our mediator that he had no way to split up his retirement fund/pension with me at that time, so he agreed I could keep the timeshare. It was just going to be an extra expense for him in the future anyway, since he would then be responsible for the annual fees that I had been making sure were paid every year—with my January bonus.

We didn't have the funds to file the divorce paperwork that day, but we were already in the process of refinancing the house to reduce the mortgage payment until we could sell it. The re-finance meant we would end up without a mortgage payment the following month, so the mediator told us we could finalize things then. We had scheduled to return to her office in October, on my mom's birthday, to execute the paperwork and pay the related fees. At that time, we would also sign over the vehicle registrations to one another, so we could each keep our own vehicle.

I remember my phone ringing during this meeting; Wayne told the mediator that it must be my boyfriend, calling to make sure I got what I wanted. She just stared at him, saying nothing, and seemed a little taken aback by the comment. I made it a point to explain to her that it was my brother, calling from Mississippi, because he was with my mom, celebrating her seventy-seventh birthday. I answered the phone, but I asked my brother if he would call me back after they had finished dinner, so I could wish my mom a *happy birthday;* and I returned to the business at hand.

The mediator asked me to verify the paperwork documented everything I had agreed to in the settlement. "Yes, it does," I replied. I couldn't help but mention also that with or without these documents, the responsibility of the upkeep with the house and the yard and the pool had already fallen solely upon me.

Wayne thought my boyfriend and I should be taking care of all the maintenance on the house and the yard now. I reiterated to Wayne—in front of the mediator—that anyone I might be spending my free time with was not responsible for our pool or our yard, but there was no point in arguing about it. He was making himself look bad enough, so there was no need for me to further point out the obvious. The paperwork was signed, the fees were paid, and the mediator said she would file the documents with the court later in the month. She said the divorce would be finalized in December, and this way we could still file a joint tax return for the year.

It was around Thanksgiving that my youngest roommate gave me her thirty day notice, and she moved back home during the Christmas break. I was thankful she had paid for the entire month of December, even though she moved out before the end of the month.

With one roommate having moved out, and the other one traveling to visit family for the holiday; Alan and I celebrated Christmas together at my house. Alan gave me a beautiful necklace. It was a white gold heart pendant, floating on a heavy sterling silver chain.

I had been wearing only sterling silver or white gold since my separation, as my former wedding ring and other jewelry were all yellow gold and reminded me too much of my years with Wayne.

I bought matching silver thumb rings for Alan and I to wear. We had begun discussing a future together; and while the divorce still wasn't actually finalized, this seemed to be a way we could show the outside world we were now a couple.

Wayne and I still had a lot of joint debt. I had filed all of our accounts with a credit counseling service, which lowered the total monthly payments and the interest rates. I advised Wayne he would have to make half of the payments until these debts were paid in full, along with half of the new mortgage payment until the housing market recovered; and we could sell our house. I was paying half of the joint debt by myself, along with my own utilities, car insurance, and other living expenses—with a little help from my room mates. The payments on the joint debt were to be made every other week, but in December, when Wayne had three pay periods; he failed to deposit his share of money into our joint account at the end of the month and told me he didn't have the money for his half of that payment! So, the payment on the debt that I had made at the end of December failed to clear the bank.

On New Year's Day, I found Wayne, sitting outside the dive bar he frequented and told him he still owed me the money for the payments. He told me it was too late; he'd already spent his paycheck.

He also informed me he'd been in a car accident the night before in the cab he'd taken home from the bar after his New Year's Eve celebrations had ended. I wanted to feel sorry for him, but I was angry.

"Karma's a bitch, huh?" I said, as I walked away.

I was so stressed as to how I was going to handle keeping my bills current for two weeks without Wayne's half of the money—especially now that my account was in the negative because of the bounced payment. Once again, Alan came to my rescue; he'd received a year-end bonus and offered to loan me the money for as long as I needed it. I was expecting a bonus myself later in January, and I told him I planned to pay him back then.

By now, Alan and I were getting more serious and had been talking about living together in the future.

I was down one roommate, and his lease was going to expire soon. I had plenty of room for his musical equipment in the room I'd originally set up for Rachel. I figured I could move her things back upstairs to the smaller room that Carey had vacated. We agreed it made more sense for him to move in and help me with the expenses at my house instead of paying for an apartment he rarely saw and often didn't feel safe in. Between his local gigs, out of town gigs, and hanging out at my house, he was only home in the late afternoons when he got off work and showered and practiced, waiting for me to get home from work.

We were spending so much time together now, it just seemed to make sense. The only hiccup was that I had yet to hear from the mediator to confirm that my divorce had been finalized the previous month.

With the way Wayne had been treating me during the last several months, I was concerned about Alan planning on moving in before the divorce was officially final; but if Alan didn't give his notice soon, he would have to sign another lease.

We determined he should go ahead and give his thirty day notice, and we would figure everything out as his move-out date approached.

I logged onto the County court website every day, looking to see if the divorce had been finalized; and on the 27th of January, the divorce was finally confirmed. The mediator had yet to be formally notified, but seeing it had been approved on the court website was good enough for me. Wayne had already terminated my health insurance with his employer as of the 1st of February anyway; so he assumed the divorce had been finalized in December, as the mediator had told us it would be. Alan officially moved in on February 1st.

Two weeks after Alan moved in, he was scheduled to fly to another city for his job, something he did twice per year; though his week long work trip the previous summer had been in Scottsdale, so he was home every night.

He surprised me one night, before he moved in, by telling me that he wanted to take me with him this time—to Nashville. I asked him why he wanted to take me on his work trip, and he told me he always had free time in the evenings and hated eating and sleeping alone; besides, it was over the Valentine's Day holiday, and he didn't want to leave me alone over such a special holiday. I was so surprised by his invitation. His job reimbursed him for his flight, hotel and meals, but he would be paying for my flight and meals.

Plus, I'd get to see Nashville, a place I had always wanted to visit.

While in Nashville, we visited friends of mine, the husband also being a musician and having his own recording studio in Nashville. They took us on a tour of his studio and to visit some of their favorite spots in the area. It was great seeing them again and visiting with their adorable twins. It was also amazing how well Alan got along with my friends, whom he had never met before.

After Alan moved in to the house, I started attending more of his gigs; not only with the band he played with locally, but also the band he played with in Prescott. It was fun, spending the weekends in Prescott, as I had points with my Marriott that I could use for hotels; and we didn't have to drive home until the following day.

The band in Prescott was a Trio; just three guys, playing alternative Rock & Roll. I liked this band as much as the band Alan played with in Phoenix; but, unfortunately, even though he and the bass player had played in bands for 20 years, their last gig with this Trio was during the summer of 2010. Now, Alan would only be playing gigs with one band, in Phoenix, though he was also still practicing with two of his friends in Mesa once a week. They weren't actually a band, but had played a couple of gigs in the past. Alan played bass with this Trio, and I hadn't even realized he played bass, too.

Unfortunately, with all of the traveling we did, I had to give up being part of the worship team at church. I had already stopped singing and was just operating the overhead projector for the songs during the service. After transferring to our customer service department at my place of employment and being on phone calls all day, my voice just couldn't handle all the practicing and singing too.

Later that year, I did start singing again though...

After seven years of not having a guitarist, I performed at the *Open Mic* night at our favorite pizza place for my 50th birthday, with Alan accompanying me on acoustic guitar and harmonies...

Chapter 22

My Rebirth

2010

Early on in our relationship, I had told Alan the story about William, our baby, and the adoption. Alan did not have any biological children of his own and once Rachel and I worked out our differences, he accepted Rachel as his *step-daughter* (even though she was now twenty years old and an adult). Alan told me I should be very proud of how I had raised Rachel; she was obviously very intelligent, hard-working, level-headed and made good decisions. He also told me if my first daughter was anything like Rachel, he was sure she had turned out just fine too. He assured me if my first daughter ever got in touch with me, he would accept her as his *step-daughter* also, because he loved me, and he would also love my children—no matter who they were.

Rachel and I had reconnected when she realized I was happy, and her dad had not been truthful about everything.

She was attending ASU and was pursuing a degree in the medical field, but she wasn't happy with her classes there. She asked me if she could move back home and go to Nursing school to get her Bachelor of Science in Nursing.

I was so excited she had decided to pursue something that she would enjoy and would give her a great career. I was happy, too, that she had accepted Alan enough to ask to move back into the house with us.

Being that my original roommate, Valerie, was still living with us in Rachel's old room and the downstairs guest room was now Alan's studio, Rachel had to move into the smaller upstairs guest room/office, but she didn't seem to mind. At the end of August, Rachel enrolled in the community college near our house for a semester to make up a class she needed in order to apply to Nursing school.

My fiftieth birthday was going to fall right before the Labor Day weekend; and I thought it would be fun to have an *old fashioned* 1960 party, complete with food and drinks popular in 1960. Alan even found a way to record the top one hundred hits from 1960. We played them on an iPod, hidden behind a retro radio. Everyone who attended dressed up in the modest styles of 1960, and we had a great time. Our favorite bartender, who had worked at the Pub where we met, was hired to make all of our *retro cocktails;* she even dressed for the era, as Bettie Page.

The following month, on October 27th, was my first daughter's thirty-second birthday. I had shared with Alan how every year I would wish my first daughter a happy birthday, by singing "Happy Birthday" to her—wherever she was.

This year, Alan hugged me tight, knowing it was still hard for me to think of that baby I had given to someone else to raise all those years ago. He was the only man who ever acknowledged how I was feeling that day, every year.

Alan and I decided to reserve my timeshare and go to Fort Lauderdale for the Christmas holiday that year, so I could show *him* where I used to live. I had scheduled the week of Christmas off work to spend at my resort because it was the only week Alan had off work each year, since his boss would close their office for the Holidays.

We had an awesome week, walking around the beach, shopping and going to several different restaurants and clubs. It was too cold to swim or sunbathe on the beach or at the pool, but just sightseeing and visiting different locations was still fun. Alan loved to walk around and check out the stores and window shop. We found an excellent restaurant open on Christmas Day, where we could eat a great lunch, and the bartender was so nice—even though he was having to work on the holiday.

Unfortunately, when I called my mom that day from Florida to wish her a Merry Christmas, she was upset that I had traveled all the way to Florida and didn't fly to Mississippi to visit my family. I tried to explain that it was cheaper to fly to Florida than to Mississippi, and we couldn't do both.

She wanted to know who I was traveling with and was even more upset when she found out I was traveling with a man, who I had been dating for over a year; and who was now living with me in Arizona. I was really hurt that she didn't even want to know his name or anything about him, because she couldn't get past the fact that we were living together! She told me I was being a bad role model for my daughter—I explained to her that Rachel was almost twenty-one years old and made her own decisions. I was hoping that seeing her mom happy and in love with a man who loved her and treated her well, would be a better example than what she had been exposed to growing up.

Alan could not understand how my mom could still get to me and upset me so much, when I was a responsible adult. He hugged me and told me everything would be fine, and we decided not to let it ruin our vacation.

My friend Rich rented our extra *studio* at my timeshare for his parents to stay in while visiting their family for Christmas, and he met Alan and took us out a couple of times also.

We ended up having a wonderful vacation; and after this trip, Alan had a better idea of my life in Florida.

I traveled with Alan twice the next year to his work related trips and enjoyed visiting places I had never seen before. It gave me a chance to read and sometimes visit with friends who lived in these cities.

During these trips, Alan and I would have breakfast before he started working, and then he would meet me each day for lunch and then go back to work. After he finished for the day, we would go out to eat dinner and check out the local entertainment in the evening.

Rachel and Marc were still dating, although long distance now, since he had moved to California for college. But she so often didn't seem happy with their relationship and to my relief, Rachel's relationship with Marc started to fizzle out after he moved out of state, and the challenges of a long distance relationship were too many to overcome. It was heart wrenching to see my daughter hurting, but I knew it was probably for the best. It was an even greater blessing when she came to the conclusion that she deserved to be treated better, with respect and kindness, especially by someone who claimed to love her.

Maybe my influences weren't all bad.

Rachel had applied for an accelerated program at the Nursing college that year and was accepted, and she had continued working part time with my employer while she attended classes. After about a year, it got to be too much to work twenty hours per week and keep up with the Nursing school classes and labs; and so Rachel had to quit and find another job she could work, just on the weekends.

Rachel and her first boyfriend, Eddie, started writing to each other the summer of 2011, while she was living at home and attending Nursing school. He was living and working in Yuma, Arizona.

At the end of the summer, our first roommate moved out and Rachel moved back into her original bedroom. We continued with our previous living arrangement throughout that year with Alan and I covering most of the bills. Rachel continued living with us while she attended the Nursing college and supported herself with a part time job.

But about this same time, Wayne decided he no longer wanted to pay for half of the mortgage—even though our daughter was living in the house while attending college. So, since it looked as though we weren't going to be able to sell our house anytime soon, we rewrote our divorce settlement; and I took over the house payment completely. In exchange, Wayne took over the remainder of the credit card debt we had two more years to make payments on.

Needless to say, he came out ahead on this deal—at least at the time—he never did have patience.

Without another roommate contributing towards the bills, the mortgage payment got to be a little much for us, and we thought about looking for another roommate. But we started cutting back on things and managed to handle all the bills with both Alan and I working full time and him playing gigs and me receiving quarterly bonuses.

It was also at this time that Alan was encouraged by his best friend, Jay, to audition to play bass for an open position in a local Blues band. Jay had been playing drums in this band for several years and, unfortunately, the bass player had recently passed away. Alan was hired to play with this band too, and so now was playing guitar with one band and bass with another, but mostly he was playing bass with the Blues band.

I missed hearing him play guitar with the cover band he had been playing with when I met him and was glad when he was playing with both bands again. These gigs kept us quite busy on the weekends, often with just one gig, but sometimes with two or three in a single weekend. I went to most, if not all, of these gigs; as I really enjoyed the music.

The following year, Alan and I were discussing me attending another one of his semi-annual work trips with him. The two of us had been a couple for over two and a half years, and I told him it felt weird to be continuously introduced as his girlfriend. I felt too old to be introduced as someone's *girlfriend*. I also told him that it often felt strange attending some gigs too; because I got the feeling some people thought I was a groupie, or just a temporary fling.

We were about to leave for a work trip to Dallas, and once again, I was dreading all of the awkward introductions.

Alan told me that he would happily introduce me as his fiancé or future wife, if we were getting married someday; but he reminded me that I had always insisted I didn't want to get married again.

I replied that after all this time, maybe I was beginning to think differently—to which he revealed that had he known my feelings toward marriage had changed, he would have asked me to marry him a long time ago.

"Is that a proposal?" I asked.

"Yes, it is." Alan replied.

"Are you serious?"

"Yes, If you want to get married, we should get married. You are the only woman I have met that I would consider marrying again!"

I didn't believe it! "You better be serious because I'm putting this on Facebook," I joked, and the two of us laughed.

"Go ahead and put it on Facebook," he said.

It might not have been the most romantic proposal, but I couldn't have been happier. My head was spinning and my heart was soaring.

I did put it on Facebook later and almost immediately had several of our friends respond with how happy they were for us!

Unfortunately, my mom had been living in a nursing home for several years and her health had recently declined because of a fall she had, and she was unable to communicate over the phone. I tried to tell her about Alan and me being engaged, but I'm not sure she understood. It was sad that my mom never got to meet Alan or see how happy I finally was. I'm sure she had spent years praying for me to find peace in my life, just as I had; and once again, my prayers had been answered.

When Alan and I arrived in Dallas, we took a walk around a beautiful pond near our hotel and discussed his proposal. We talked about possible wedding dates, and realized we needed to schedule something soon as Alan was still playing in two different bands, and his gig calendar was filling up quickly. Alan knew my favorite number had always been *twelve* and thought I might want to get married on the twelfth day of a month. But he also had reservations, because the last time I got married on that day, things had ended badly.

"It's true," I said. "But there are eleven other months in the year to pick from." And then I came up with an absolutely perfect wedding date. "How about 12/12/12?" I suggested. "Is that a Saturday?" Alan asked.

"I don't know, but who says you have to get married on a Saturday?" I replied.

The 12th of December was actually going to fall on a Wednesday. This made the date even more perfect; most likely, we wouldn't have to try to schedule our wedding around Alan's gig schedule (since most of the time, his bands only performed on weekends).

We took a picture of ourselves together on a bench by the pond that afternoon—one that ended up on our *Save the Date* announcements.

All of our friends were excited for us—and a little surprised we were going to get married on a Wednesday evening. But even so, almost everyone confirmed that they would be there. I spent our trip making wedding plans, figuring out the guest list, and designing the invitations.

When we returned home, I realized, looking through my guest list, that I had many friends who were going to be guests who I could also hire to help with our wedding. This made everything so much more personal because everyone involved with our wedding was already a friend of ours. We only needed to find someone to perform the ceremony.

Alan and I were busy back at work and Rachel was busy in Nursing school, when we received a call from Edward one morning in April that my mom had passed away in her sleep.

Rachel and I took off for a few days and flew to Mississippi to attend my mom's funeral. We were able to meet up with Jordan in Texas on the way. We arrived in Jackson, and the three of us met up with my cousin, Lynn; and all of us rode together to Northern Mississippi.

When we attended my mom's viewing at the church, I was surprised at how small she had become; she weighed less than 100 pounds when she passed. But I also knew she passed on from this earth into heaven in her sleep and was no longer in any pain. She was at peace, watching over all of us.

We spent a few days in Mississippi at Edward's house, visiting the only family we had left on my side, Edward, his wife, their four children, and Jordan.

When we returned to Arizona, Rachel continued in Nursing school and writing to Eddie, and I returned to work and planning Alan's and my wedding.

Rachel and Eddie had been writing to each other for over a year when he moved back to his Dad's house in Fountain Hills.

He stayed with his dad for about a week, and Rachel spent most of that week with them. After his visit, the two of them asked me if Eddie could move in with us. He had already landed a job in downtown Phoenix, which was only a twenty-minute drive from our house. I hadn't really realized when Eddie moved back to town that he and Rachel were back together as a *couple*—it had been seven years since they had dated in high school. Alan and I agreed to let him live with us also, and he moved into our guest room/office. Alan did not know Eddie, and he wasn't sure about him living with us; but he accepted that if Rachel and I liked him and trusted him, he would like him and trust him too.

All four of us were busy working, and Rachel was attending college too; but we made it a point to get together for dinner at least once a week to check in with each other. Eddie had grown up quite a bit during their time apart, and he and Rachel were getting along really well; I was so happy to see them together again. We didn't ask Eddie to pay rent because he had several bills he was trying to pay off and wanted to get out of debt as quickly as possible. He helped with the yard and pool work at the house and paid for all of his and Rachel's bills when she had to resign from working to concentrate solely on school.

The atmosphere in our house was so different from what it used to be when Rachel lived at home during high school.

There was no yelling, no fighting, and no crying—it was mellow and relaxing to be at home now.

Alan and I decided to hold our wedding ceremony and reception at our house. Alan had a friend and fellow musician who's wife, Jane, did a little party planning, and she helped me get some ideas together for decorating the yard for the wedding. Jane also helped me plan the menu and was put in charge of the food for the reception. We *hired* a few of Rachel's best friends to assist with the wedding too. I hired my long time friend, Patricia, who had been cleaning my house for years and was also an excellent seamstress and baker, to help me with the wedding too. If she could help me get the house ready and make my wedding cake, those were two things I could scratch off of my to do list.

Working full time and trying to plan a wedding left me little time to consider sewing my own wedding dress, but I knew I wanted my dress to be unconventional—I wanted to feel like a princess, and I had to wear a tiara. As for the dress, I thought I found the perfect one while searching the internet. It was a long, formal gown; and since our wedding colors were going to be holiday themed (black and white with red and green), I chose the dress in jade green satin and chiffon with black lace accents. The guys would be wearing black pants, white button down shirts, and jade green satin ties.

To my dismay, when the dress arrived in November, the sizing was all wrong; and the dress was huge on me. I decided to go shopping for another dress—as soon as I could find the time—but when Patricia found out about my dilemma, she offered to work her magic. After her alterations, the dress fit perfectly. Patricia played such an important role in so many aspects of our wedding, and I was very thankful for her contributions. She was obviously an answer to my prayers!

Since our wedding was already unconventional, I had designed the invitations to look like back stage passes. The event schedule began with a 5 pm *happy hour* with live music—performed by a couple of solo artists we knew. As the guests arrived and signed our guestbook, each of them wrote their name on a white plastic wine cup or red plastic beer cup, with the benefit of serving as a sort of name tag also.

Another friend of ours and fellow musician, Mike, had recently been ordained and was going to perform the ceremony. Just before the wedding began, he played an electric guitar solo with Alan, playing bass and Alan's best man, Jay, playing drums. The guests began moving away from the patio towards the back half of our yard, where the fire pit was blazing to keep everyone warm. Once the prelude was finished, Alan and Jay lowered a float with dry ice on it into the pool, adding to the ambiance of our venue.

Mike placed his electric guitar on a stand and walked over to the spa area of the pool and picked up an acoustic guitar. He played, "At Last," while our friend, Marie, sang along; and the groom and best man moved to their places on the pool deck.

Rachel served as my maid of honor, and the two of us exited the house through the back French doors. We walked around the pool to our places and stood in front of the crowd of guests—close to one hundred and fifty people—ready to begin the ceremony.

When the processional song ended, Mike put his acoustic guitar on its stand and stepped over to the music stand between Alan and me and began to officiate. He had chosen a ceremony with all musical related phrases about harmony and being *in tune* with each other. This was the first wedding ceremony he had performed, and he wanted it to be perfect.

I had written two pages of vows for the ceremony but could barely get through the first page without crying. Then it was Alan's turn. He had written just a few lines, but they were from his heart and meant the world to me. "Neither of us is perfect, but we're perfect for each other," Alan's words rang so true for me. He always accepted me and never criticized me, even with all my flaws.

After we were pronounced husband and wife, the party continued. We served appetizers, beer, and wine and it was one big celebration; a six hour long *happy hour*.

We featured a total of six musical groups—two solos, two duos, and two bands. Even the Blues band that Alan played with performed a few songs (that I got to choose); but not until after we had danced our first dance, and our cake had been cut. I hadn't planned on Alan having to *work* at our wedding; but the band said that this was their gift to me, and I happily accepted.

I also had the opportunity to sing a couple of songs with the last two groups, and the night came to a close right around eleven—thankfully, without any complaints to the police for excessive noise. It was the perfect wedding—for us—a magical, music-filled evening.

While I watched Rachel and Eddie help clean up and shut down things at the end of the night, I couldn't help but wonder about my first daughter. I would have loved for her to have attended this magical evening, but I still didn't know where she was—or even who she was. Was she married now? Did I have grandchildren? I knew it was in God's hands whether or not these questions would ever be answered.

I only took a few days off work for our wedding, wanting to save my vacation days for our honeymoon—which was scheduled for later in the month.

I had already booked my timeshare a year in advance for us to revisit Fort Lauderdale, since Alan and I had spent a week vacationing there in December a couple of years earlier; and we discovered we really liked it there during December. Now it was coordinating almost perfectly with our wedding date. Unfortunately, Alan's gig calendar had been filling up, so we were going to have to leave Florida a couple of days earlier than originally planned.

I was quickly learning what it was going to be like to be married to a working musician.

Alan and I still ended up having a wonderful honeymoon; and while it was still too cold to swim in the ocean or the resort pool, we managed to get plenty of time outdoors, walking in the sunshine, shopping, visiting restaurants and listening to live music.

Our friend, Rich, also visited us for a couple of days and took us out to dinner to celebrate our marriage. It seems I had lost touch with everyone else I knew from my high school days in Florida and had only been able to find Rich because of Facebook.

Chapter 23

Lifestyle changes

2013

At the start of the new year, Alan's boss sold their business location, and Alan began working from home the following month. Alan started not only running his business from home, but also managed to do all the work that needed done at the house. He began doing most of the grocery shopping and made most of our meals also. I was so blessed and felt so much less stress, even though I was still working full time; because Alan took care of many of the things at home that needed to be done while I was gone for work 10-12 hours per day.

During that summer, Rachel graduated from the Nursing college. Alan and I attended her graduation, along with Wayne and his girlfriend and Eddie and several of their friends. We were all invited to go out together after the ceremony, but her Dad and his girlfriend did not show up. Rachel introduced Alan and me to all of her school friends.

We planned a graduation party at the house for the following weekend; and it was so nice to have a house full of friendly kids, mostly nurses, enjoying the pool and having a good time—relieved to be done with school!

Having Alan working from home also turned out to be a blessing in disguise that year, as I ended up in the hospital three times. Having a daughter who was officially a nurse now also helped.

My first hospitalization had been planned, but delayed because of our wedding. I took off two weeks to recover, and Alan was home and able to help me out, when needed. But one weekend, six months later, while Alan was playing at an out of town gig; I was bit by a spider. I didn't realize how serious the bite was until a few days later when it abscessed, while we were out of town, celebrating a friend's birthday. I ended up having surgery twice to remove infected tissue. It was amazing how something so unexpected could happen that would send me to a hospital emergency room and turn into five days in the hospital, hooked up to a morphine IV, that I again was reminded how very fragile life could be.

A few weeks after Rachel's graduation, she was hired at a top-ranked Children's Hospital in the city. About the same time, she and Eddie decided to find their own place to live. Now Alan and I were alone in the house; and while I missed my daughter's presence, it was nice to finally be able to have available space for all of Alan's things.

His music studio remained on the first floor, but he converted one of the upstairs bedrooms into a home office.

Rachel's room was made into a guest room for any family or friends needing a place to stay.

We had been invited to attend Jordan's wedding and reception in Northern California that September, after I was released from the hospital, but had not planned on attending because of work and finances, and now my hospitalization. I really was sad to have to decline the invitation (and our chance to meet Jordan's new wife).

Jordan and his wife were planning on moving to Europe after their honeymoon, so Jordan could continue his education; but they surprised us and spent their honeymoon, traveling to Southern California and to Arizona to visit friends and relatives. They stayed a couple of nights with us before they headed back home to Northern California to prepare for their trip to Europe. It was so nice to see what an amazing young man my nephew had become and also what an amazing young lady his wife was. This also gave them a chance to meet Alan.

As the year went by, I started thinking more about my first daughter again—now that Jordan was married and Rachel and Eddie were a couple. I also started feeling more like I was a grandmother. Most of our friends were grandparents by now, and it seemed likely my oldest daughter was married with children.

But as Alan had no biological children of his own, and Rachel and Eddie were not planning on having any children soon; I began to wonder more about this possibility. Something in my heart told me she had to have children by now, but I left it up to God to reveal this to me someday.

Rachel and Eddie's relationship continued to progress…

After working full time and living together in their condo for a year, and being *parents* of two dogs; they decided to look for a *fixer-upper* with a big yard for their dogs. They found just what they were looking for, only three miles away from us. With the help of family and friends—and a lot of hard work—Rachel and Eddie turned their new (27 year old) house into a beautiful home. I discovered that Rachel had a lot of design sense, and I assumed a little of it was a trait she acquired from me. I'd always been interested in home décor and Interior Design and remodeling; and she had helped me choose our home furnishings, a lot, even when she was very young. I was very proud of the home she and Eddie had created and how well they were taking care of it.

Eddie's best friend, Ryan, had moved in with them; but talks were leaning toward Eddie and Rachel getting married and having children in the near future; so they figured they might need that extra room, someday, when they started a family. While they were not yet even engaged, Eddie's mother and I were certain Eddie had a plan.

They talked about marriage often, and we were waiting to see how Eddie was going to surprise Rachel—someday— and propose. For now, we would just have to wait *patiently*.

In the meantime, after years of not hearing from William, having last seen him during my vacation to Fort Lauderdale with Wayne when Rachel was a child; William reached out to me on Facebook.

I couldn't help but acknowledge that without modern technology, it would have been terribly difficult for us to have reconnected. It had taken me many attempts the last time around to get a message to him, and for him to contact me in return. William and I said our "hello's" on Facebook, but we never really communicated on a regular basis. I'd sent him a couple of messages, wondering if he had ever found a possible connection between our daughter and his dad's family here, in Arizona.

Since I had learned that William's grandmother had assisted in the adoption of our daughter on his side, I had questioned whether he had ever asked his family if they had any information regarding the adoption. But William never responded. Unfortunately, this just added to my suspicions that someone in his family possibly knew who our daughter was or where she was.

The following year, Alan and I decided to take Rachel and Eddie with us to Florida for a ten-night, three-city adventure. We had to schedule this vacation a year in advance also because by now, Alan was playing part time in 2 more bands—and he and Jay were forming their own band also. I wanted to get the dates confirmed before any gigs were booked in any of the 5 bands in which Alan was playing.

I also reached out to William to let him know when we would be in Florida, and asked him if he'd like to meet up with us all while we were visiting. I didn't know what part of Florida he was currently living in, but I told him we would be in Fort Lauderdale, Key West, and then Hollywood. As it turned out, he was living in Hollywood; he said he would meet with us there.

We were only going to be in Hollywood for the last three nights of our vacation, and I contacted William several times before we left for Florida to try to schedule something. When we arrived in Hollywood, I invited him first to a pizza place in the area that had been highly recommended, but he was unable to meet us that evening. We only had two more nights, and so I asked him if he wanted to choose the restaurant and thought we'd just meet him at a local taco shop or somewhere close by; but that didn't work either.

We had made plans to spend our last night we were in Florida at a restaurant that also featured live music. I invited William to join us. He finally arrived after we had finished eating; and after introductions, Rachel and Eddie went to play pool. William and Alan and I sat and talked for a while. The band started shortly afterwards, which made conversation difficult. William hadn't let on that he had any new information about our daughter, but instead told me he had some leads and would let me know if he found out anything. He explained a little about his leads to us, but with the music so loud, I heard very little of the details. In the end, I figured at least my family finally got to meet William. William again promised to stay in touch. This time, he kept his promise.

Throughout several email conversations, he told me he was trying to get information from his mom; his grandmother had since passed away, and her files were transferred to the firm that acquired her practice. He told me his mom claimed she didn't remember any of the details, which made me more suspicious; but he told me, unfortunately, her memory was not all it used to be. I wasn't sure why William hadn't talked to his mom or grandmother about this when he was younger.

William's biological father lived in Arizona with his second family, and he had a daughter close to our daughter's age.

They only lived a half hour away from us, close to where Rachel had spent much of her time at her best friend's house in Fountain Hills. I kept asking William about his Dad's daughter, and if he knew when her birthdate was; but he said he didn't remember. I hated to be suspicious, but I still felt he had information he wasn't sharing with me. I also found out that William had come to Arizona several times to visit his dad and his second family, but he never got in touch with me. He said he didn't know how to reach me back then and since he had contacted me, he had only been to Arizona for short, event filled weekends.

I heard from William a couple of times over the next few months, and he said he was still trying to get information that might help us find our daughter. Even though he had progressed from messaging me on Facebook to sending me e-mails; I gave him my phone number, so he could call me or text me, if needed.

If William was unable to access the information from his grandmother's legal files, I didn't know what more he could do that I hadn't already tried to do myself. Years before, I had been told that private adoptions in Mississippi were sealed files, and the child had to find the biological parents; the biological parents would not likely be able to find the child. I kept hoping and praying that William's mother would remember some information that her mother had passed on to her, but she never did.

I did thank him for trying, but at this point, I'd put it all in God's hands years earlier; if my first daughter was meant to find me, she would. I didn't know William's family well, so I wasn't really convinced they were helping him look for our daughter; but he told me he had a cousin, on his mother's side, who kept in contact with everyone. Her family was in charge of the *family tree*. I wondered if this was the family who had told me about William's biological father years earlier, but I thought that was someone on his father's side of the family—so I wasn't sure who this *cousin* was.

William contacted me a few more times during the next year, just to check in with me. He also let me know that his cousin, Pauline, was now helping him try to find our daughter. She had been compiling their family history, William hoped her research would somehow lead her to our daughter. I didn't quite understand how this was going to happen—unless our daughter was looking for us.

It was near the end of the year—December 3rd to be exact —that I received a text from William. It only said, "Are you home?"

"Yes," I replied.

Chapter 24

New technology

2016

"You better sit down for this one."

"Are you sitting down?" William texted.

"Yes, William, I am sitting down."

"What now?" I replied.

"I think Pauline might have found our daughter!"

I was stunned, I didn't know how to respond; I just sat on my bed, staring at the wall.

William continued to text me…

He texted that Pauline had been on an ancestry website and recently submitted a DNA test in an effort to find other relatives in their family. Of course, connections were dependent on those other relatives being on the same ancestry site and also submitting DNA tests. I hadn't known this particular website had been using such testing, and so it never occurred to me that someone might use the site to locate their biological parents.

I didn't even know if our daughter had been told she was adopted, though I had prayed she was. Still, the chance of finding our daughter this way didn't sound likely to me, but I supposed it was possible. But now that William was telling me this process might have worked, I was in complete shock.

I was on my way out of the house for an evening gig with Alan and since this kind of seemed like it could be another random text from William, though a little more extreme than previous texts, I didn't think to just call him and find out what was going on—I was also *afraid* of finding out what he actually had discovered.

I wondered why William's family had helped him try to locate our daughter and not mine? Why did he find the connection to our daughter and not me?

William continued to text me throughout the evening and told me that the ancestry website matched Pauline with a possible second cousin. When she found out that this unknown second cousin was a female, born in the same year as our daughter and adopted in Mississippi; Pauline explained to the girl that she might know her biological father.

Later, Pauline shared with me that she had actually told William that she had been connected with a female, born on his daughter's birthdate—now living in Florida but born in Mississippi and privately adopted at birth.

William was certain this was our daughter and asked Pauline if she could give this girl his email address, perhaps ask if she would send pictures of herself either as a child or an adult. The woman's name was Gayle, and she agreed to email pictures of herself, both as an adult and a young child, to Pauline and William. The resemblance to William's side of the family was uncanny, he said, especially in her childhood photographs. William and Pauline were convinced this was our daughter.

William offered to forward the pictures to me and give me Gayle's email address, but he was so convinced that she was our daughter, he called me first to let me know that Gayle wanted to email me too. When I hung up the phone, my head was spinning. All of this had been going on between William, Pauline, and a woman who could turn out to be our daughter. I had been praying about this for years; was it possible that once again, God would answer my prayers?

I was astonished. It had been over thirty-eight years since I gave birth to my first daughter; and after waiting for so long, everything seemed to be happening too fast now. But of course, I wanted to see her photographs.

I expected Gayle to look similar to me and Rachel but perhaps with William's dark curly hair—instead of being blonde, like the two of us.

The thought that Rachel might finally, someday, be able to meet her sister made this all the more real and exciting.

My heart was pounding as I opened the email and began to click on the photos…

Gayle looked nothing like me, and nothing like Rachel; in fact she didn't look at all like what I had imagined she might look like! But I could definitely see similarities between Gayle and William's half sister (who I still had my suspicions about since I had found out about her existence).

Gayle was an adorable child, and a beautiful young adult woman. Her style of dress was much more conservative than mine and Rachel's. She definitely looked like someone who had been raised in a traditional, conservative Christian environment—like the one I'd known in Mississippi. I showed the pictures to Alan and to Rachel, and they agreed with me that she looked like William, but bore little, if any, resemblance to me.

Rachel could not understand how she and I could look so similar, but I could have another daughter that didn't look anything like either of us. I told Rachel and Alan that because of William's heritage, his genes were obviously more dominant than mine; and that would explain why she had dark, thick, curly hair and darker skin than we did. They understood this, but still thought she would look at least a little bit like me.

As I processed these things, suspicions crept into my head, and I began to wonder if perhaps this was some kind of scam.

I'd always been a little suspicious of William's family and wondered how much his Grandmother had been involved in the adoption. Especially when I found out he had a half sister who I felt looked like what our daughter might look like! Now, his cousin was telling us she found a DNA match to his family, in Florida. But why would they want to fool me? Were they hiding something? Did William have another child with someone else, and these were her pictures? Were these pictures of another one of his family members that I didn't know? I needed to know more. I was just so confused. William asked me to email Gayle directly so we could communicate, and so I did...

Gayle-

So, where do I start? I was contacted by William last night and he told me that his cousin, Pauline, had a DNA match with you on an ancestry site. She contacted him because she knew he was looking for his biological daughter who had been adopted in 1978. I guess I am in shock because William and I only recently (within the last year) started really communicating again. He told me he had family members helping him locate our daughter, but I really didn't understand what he could be doing that I hadn't already tried to do in the past.

293

I am also surprised to find out that you live in Florida (where William lives and where I used to live).

I knew this day would come-someday-I guess I just never thought about what I would do when it did!

I hate to sound skeptical, but I need to have more information to connect the dots. (Though William says the pictures you sent look a lot like he and his sister as children and now).

I have seen a recent picture of you and I do think that you look very similar to William's sister—though I've never met her in person.

Can you tell me more about your parents (and did you know you were adopted as a child)? What were your parents occupations and hobbies? Did they attend a church? If so, where?

I only have limited information about the family that adopted my baby, but I did live in Mississippi in 1978, and I did have a daughter that was adopted by a couple there. My mom's family lived in Mississippi—which is why we moved there.

You can email me if you want to-I think this would be much easier than talking on the phone at this point.

My name is Eliza Beth, and I live in Phoenix AZ.

Later that same day, I received an email reply from Gayle...

Eliza Beth-

This is overwhelming, right? I don't even know where to begin—William is so sure that the DNA test on the ancestry site is scientific, but it all seems surreal at this point.

I want you to know that I have had the most wonderful life and I could not be more grateful for the decision my biological parents made to give a couple the privilege of parenthood. I was (and still am) the center of my parent's world and couldn't be more thankful for all they have done and continue to do for me. They are truly amazing people. My parents told me from a young age that I was adopted and always made it mean that I was 'extra special' which was such a wise handling of the situation. I did not face a lot of the questions that many adoptive children have.

On the practical side, I am going to request that William take a scientific paternity test that would confirm this to be a 100% positive match. I think that would just be best for everyone to not have any questions on that front.

The DNA test I am looking at has a three way testing option that I could send to you as well, if you would like. This is something I am paying for, and I will leave that up to you if you want to take the test also.

I don't know a lot about my biological parents, and I don't think my parents know a lot about them either, but this is what I've been told. By the way, I have not shared this information with William because it would probably only apply to you.

I was born on October 27, 1978, outside of Jackson Mississippi. I believe the name of the hospital was The Women's Hospital and my mother and the biological mother shared the same doctor. I was told he helped arrange the adoption.

I was also told that my biological father's grandmother was an attorney and handled the legal paperwork on his side. I know that both of my parents were young, and I was told that somewhere along the way, my biological mother asked for a Christian couple to adopt her baby.

I'm not sure if this information helps you at all, but I am guessing that you are the one with the most facts about the situation and will know if this information matches up to your memories.

-Gayle

Even though this information was accurate, I thought about it and realized I could have told William most of this in the past, or his grandmother could have mentioned it to him; so I was still not one hundred percent convinced.

A couple of days later I was at work when I received another email from Gayle.

She asked if I had thought further about taking the DNA test, and if so, if I would send her my address; so she could have the test sent to me. She also included some additional information for me regarding her adoption in Mississippi. Included in her second email were the ages of her parents at the time of the adoption, their occupations, and some of their hobbies. These details matched, exactly, with what I knew about the couple who had adopted my baby girl!

She explained that her biological mother and her adoptive mother had shared the same OB/GYN doctor, and he knew of a couple who really wanted a baby—this is how they found out about me. She shared with me that her mother could not have children of her own and had suffered several miscarriages. Finally, she told me that her parents had been on a five-year waiting list to adopt a baby when they were told about my baby.

Gayle probably didn't realize it when she sent this email, but she ended up telling me exactly what I needed to hear to connect her to the daughter I had given to a couple to adopt all those years earlier.

I sat at my desk, reading this email over and over and began to cry.

I was having a hard time concentrating on work or trying to keep my emotions in check, but it wasn't as though I could leave work and go home over an email. So I took a short break from my duties, and I wrote back to Gayle. I told her I was in tears, reading her email over and over, and I was now convinced that she was my daughter—even without the paternity/maternity DNA tests. And if she was my daughter, then William was her biological father, because our child was the only one I had given birth to and given to someone else to raise.

Gayle responded to me that she was also in tears, just reading my email response. But she still wanted us all to be 100% sure and take the DNA tests, and I could hardly blame her. She still really had no idea who we were before this DNA connection had been made. So, I agreed to take the DNA test, and she arranged for them to be sent to us right away. We all did the tests in our homes the following week and sent them off to the lab. All of us were curious, but I knew in my heart that she was my daughter.

A week or so later, the tests results came back to Gayle and she mailed a copy to each of us. The results were 99.9% positive that we were her parents, and she was our daughter!

She might not have looked much like me; but she had turned out exactly how I had prayed she would, so many years before, when I signed the adoption papers.

Gayle was raised by a wonderful Christian couple, well educated and successful. She was brought up with music all around her and had played piano most of her childhood. She was loved just like she was her parents' biological child and was the center of their world.

Gayle was now happily married to an awesome man, Dean; both she and Dean were lawyers. Not surprising at all, they also had three young children. She had not given birth to her first child until she was age thirty, and now my question had been answered—I was, indeed, a grandmother—just not until I was forty-eight years old (the year Wayne and I had taken the girls to Florida and then separated).

Over the course of the next several weeks, we exchanged numerous emails, beginning the process of sharing information about ourselves and our lives. Gayle told me a little about her past, her education, and her occupation; and I shared the same with her. Strangely enough, she told me three of her favorite things were coffee, red wine, and interior design; which were three of my favorite things also. She said her parents had always told her she was adopted and that meant she was very special, and she had been treated like a princess.

For me, this was another answered prayer.

Gayle wanted to know how she had *come about* and more about my relationship with her biological father, William.

I asked her how much of the story she really wanted to hear, and she said she wanted to hear as much as I wanted to share. I told her a little about how we met, how long we knew each other, the night she was conceived, and how I learned of her existence. I also shared with her how I had come to my decision to have her, even though the doctor who had told me I was pregnant with her had also advised that I should not have her. Then I explained why I had given her to someone else to raise.

With each email exchanged, we both ended up in tears.

I learned that her family had left Mississippi when she was just two years old and moved to Tennessee and then moved back to Mississippi—to Brookhaven—when she was eight years old. Her favorite part of town when she was growing up was Whitworth College campus, ironically, the school I had attended when I was pregnant with her. It was also where I had lived while she was an infant in Jackson, just an hour away.

I also learned that she and her husband met during law school while they were in Phoenix, attending seminars and had stayed in a hotel on the same road as my office building—just two and half miles away. She had even, most likely, shopped at the store that William's biological father managed.

It seemed God had always kept us close, even if we hadn't known it at the time.

Chapter 25

Making up for lost time

2017

William wanted to meet up with Gayle and her husband in person, as soon as possible; so it was decided that Gayle and Dean would drive to Fort Lauderdale the following month, which was about a three hour drive from their home in the Orlando area. They planned to stay in Fort Lauderdale for the weekend and meet William and his girlfriend for dinner. William also planned to have the rest of his family meet them—to include his mother, brother, niece and nephew; along with William's cousin, Pauline, who had been responsible for locating Gayle. Luckily, Dean came from a large family and had four siblings, three with spouses and two couples with children, so it wasn't too over-whelming for Gayle to be in the midst of such a large family gathering, in spite of the fact that she had grown up as an only child.

I was sent pictures of the family gathering from both Gayle and William. It was both heartwarming and heartbreaking. I felt like I had spent more time than anyone over the years thinking about, and trying to find, our daughter; and I wished I could have been the first to meet her. But William only lived a few hours from Gayle; I was a four to five hour cross country flight away.

At the time, Alan and I could not afford to take off time from our jobs right away and fly to Florida—even for just a weekend. Besides, I really wanted to spend more time with Gayle and Dean than just a weekend, and I wanted to meet our grandchildren, too. But as God always has a way of working things out for the best, He would be providing a time and place for all of us to meet.

A few months after Gayle and Dean met William and his family in Fort Lauderdale, other family members from William's biological father's family were flying to Florida from Arizona for William's niece's wedding. They made plans to drive up after the wedding to the Orlando area, so they could also meet Gayle and Dean—and their children. Once again, I was feeling really left out. This was the child who had survived inside of me, unbeknownst to anyone, for months, through a near-death experience—the child I had been praying for my entire adult life. I'd spent years trying to find her, unsuccessfully, eventually having no choice but to let go and turn it over to God. But I realized I was being selfish; I didn't blame them for wanting to meet Gayle—it had been thirty-eight years, and William's parents were not getting any younger. I was still going to be Gayle's biological mother, no matter how many other family members got to meet her in person before I did.

I was saddened that my own parents, already deceased, would not get to share in this awesome experience, but I felt as though they had been watching over us all along.

One day, they would meet her, in heaven.

Again, I had to exercise patience.

Originally, William met with Gayle in January, but we were going to have to wait until July; when we would be traveling to Orlando for Alan's work. In reality, this was another prayer answered, because otherwise we probably would not have been able to afford the trip to Florida until our already reserved September vacation week in Fort Lauderdale that year. In the meantime, we would have to get to know each other by other means.

Gayle, Dean, and I began exchanging emails and sending pictures of ourselves and our families to each other. Once we got to know each other a little better, we started texting.

In May, we had planned a weekend day to call each other and talk over the phone. It felt like Gayle and I were already friends as soon as we started talking and sharing stories. That first phone conversation was over two and a half hours long. I was so excited that in less than two months, we would be meeting face to face.

The weeks seemed to crawl by, but finally July arrived, and we began our travels. We made plans to meet Gayle and Dean for dinner the first night we arrived, and while we had scheduled to meet at 7pm; flight delays, luggage delays, car rental and hotel check in, caused us to arrive two hours late!

I was a little stressed over our late arrival, but Gayle assured me that she and Dean had been enjoying a *date night* out alone, having drinks and appetizers, when we finally did arrive. Once seated at the table, it felt like we were meeting with family we had already known for years.

We talked just like we were old friends; the months we'd spent emailing and texting and sending photos had really helped us to get to know each other. Gayle and Dean gave us their schedules for the time we would be there, and we coordinated meeting with them—and their families and friends—as much as possible.

We learned that Dean and Gayle would both be working some during the week and Dean would be going out of town at the end of it; Gayle would be driving three hours to Tallahassee the following Monday for a job interview for her dream job. But for now, we were going to be spending the 4th of July at Dean's parent's house with a few of their family members and at their best friends' house, watching fireworks. The family we would be meeting was, unfortunately, not the couple who had adopted Gayle as a baby, as they still lived in Mississippi—and I don't think they were ready to meet me yet. We would however, be meeting Dean's parents, the very ones who had encouraged Gayle to learn about her heritage on the ancestry website to satisfy her curiosity. We would also meet Dean's brothers and their families; unfortunately, his two sisters were unable to be home that day.

Another connection came when we found out that one of Gayle's sisters-in-law was from Arizona and had gone to high school with a couple of Rachel's friends, one of them being Allie, and they were all connected through Facebook!

Everyone was so nice, and so happy to meet us—they really made me feel so special. Dean's mom and dad reminded me so much of my Aunt Lora and Uncle Harold, who had also been a minister, that we felt totally at home in their house.

We enjoyed a great potluck style meal and spent the afternoon out on the patio, watching the grandchildren play in the pool, talking and then taking pictures. The seven of us left Dean's parent's house in the late afternoon and headed out to watch fireworks at a home that belonged to Gayle's and Dean's best friends.

Their best friends' house was beautiful, professionally designed and decorated, which I absolutely loved. I wanted to ask for a tour, but that wasn't why I was there; I was there to meet all these friends of the daughter I never knew —until now. The couple and their children were so kind to open up their house, patio and pool to many of their friends, and it gave us the opportunity to relax and talk while the kids were swimming again. Their home was on lakefront property, and we enjoyed multiple fireworks shows across the water from the back yard.

Alan and I felt like we already knew these people, because they were all friends of Gayle's and Dean's, and they treated us like we were family—which, I guess, we were. Before the fireworks started, the sun crept below the horizon at the edge of the lake, void of any boats at the time, but the sky was full of colors. It was the most gorgeous sunset I had ever seen, although perhaps it just felt that way because I was so happy and everything seemed so perfect.

During the rest of our time in the Orlando area, Gayle brought the grandkids over to swim in the pools at the hotels where we were staying. Gayle and Dean took us out to eat several times, too. We also enjoyed more fireworks shows—a nightly event in Orlando. Gayle even treated me to an afternoon at the spa in the resort where we were staying.

That same day Gayle also left for her dream job interview in Tallahassee, which was the following morning. This was an important position for which twenty people had applied, but only six of the applicants were being interviewed; and we were all praying for Gayle to do her best.

When she returned to Orlando the following evening, she once again met Alan and me for dinner, along with the grandchildren, so we could say our goodbyes.

After dinner, we walked around, listened to music, took pictures and then we all hugged each other goodbye, comforted in the knowledge we would see each other again soon. It was such an amazing vacation, I don't think the experience could have been much better. I left, hoping we would have the opportunity to come back and see all of these people again and meet the rest of Dean's family—and maybe even Gayle's adoptive parents, someday.

Alan and I spent one last night at our hotel and flew back to Phoenix the next day.

I couldn't express how thankful I was, after over thirty-eight years of prayers, I had finally met my oldest daughter and her amazing family.

Chapter 26

A reunion with new family and friends

Alan and I had previously scheduled a vacation to return to Fort Lauderdale in September with Rachel and Eddie. We had experienced so much fun two years before with them in Florida, we thought we would do it again—this time, staying just in Fort Lauderdale. But having ended up taking extra time off to spend in Orlando in July to meet Gayle and her family, we decided we couldn't afford another vacation so soon and were considering selling my week at the Marriott to Rich or someone else. I hadn't wanted to cancel on Rachel and Eddie though, but the two of them ended up canceling on us; Eddie had finally proposed, and they were now saving their money for their upcoming wedding.

Eddie had surprised Rachel while they were in Monterey, CA, visiting family and taking a walk on the beach one evening at sunset. He had even found a way to record the entire proposal! It was a one of a kind proposal—just what we would have expected from Eddie.

I was unable to sell our week at the Marriott so late in the year, so Alan and I decided to go ahead and spend my birthday week in Florida.

I asked Gayle and Dean if they would like to drive down to Fort Lauderdale with the grandchildren and spend a few days on the beach with us over the long holiday weekend. The kids were already in school, but it wasn't too long of a drive from their home, so they agreed. They arrived in Fort Lauderdale early Saturday.

They spent the day at the resort and the beach, waiting for our flight to arrive that evening. That Saturday just so happened to also be my birthday, and I couldn't imagine a better birthday gift than to spend more time with my first daughter, her husband, and my grandchildren.

Gayle picked Alan and I up at the airport and took us back to the resort, where we walked over to one of our favorite little restaurants at the resort mall and met Dean and the children. The children had already eaten; but Dean and the kids saved the table, so we could meet them there. They stayed with us for a while and wished me a *Happy Birthday* before heading back to the room with Dean.

The next day, we all had an awesome breakfast at another one of our favorite restaurants and then headed to the beach, where the kids swam and played in the water and Gayle and I talked, while my youngest grandchild buried our feet in the sand. The water was so calm that the kids were fine to play by themselves at the edge of the water—and even a few feet in—even the youngest, at age 2, was having a great time.

I had planned to take Gayle and my new family out to my favorite restaurant, in the area where I used to live with Leigh, on Sunday evening, and she had asked if she could invite William and his girlfriend to join us. As it turned out, William's mom's birthday was just two days after mine, so we invited her to come along as well. I hadn't seen his mother since high school—I figured that this was going to be an interesting evening.

Now that we had included William's mom in our dinner, it seemed we should also invite William's brother, George, and his family. When all was said and done, our dinner party had grown to thirteen adults, one teenager, two young children, and a toddler in a highchair. This was definitely going to be a once in a lifetime gathering; we would be celebrating two birthdays, Gayle's new dream job she had been offered (that she would be starting when she returned home), and a gathering of four generations of William's family. The evening was beyond memorable, with a great dinner and interesting conversations—and me, still in amazement at being in the presence of my oldest daughter, who sat between me and William's mom.

Dean and William kept the grandchildren entertained at the other end of the table.

Best of all, we managed to gather everyone outside to take family photos before dinner—before the sun set, memorializing this gathering of these four generations of family. After dinner, half of us continued the party at a nearby outdoor bar by the beach, and then we found a night club with live music and dancing. It was a wonderful evening, and one of the best birthday weekends I'd ever had.

It was also hurricane season, and storms were expected to hit Fort Lauderdale by the end of the following week. I wasn't concerned though; Alan had a gig back in Arizona that following Saturday, so we would be leaving on Friday evening, before the storms arrived.

I'd spent such a large part of my life in Florida, the news of a hurricane wasn't too worrisome; it was far out in the Atlantic, and at any rate, we'd be gone before it made landfall.

On Monday morning, Gayle and Dean and the kids and I went to the beach again. By now, the waves had begun to stir up more seaweed and the ocean was no longer calm enough for the children to play in the water alone. The lifeguard told us that the adults would have to accompany the children in the water; but we didn't mind, as we weren't staying at the beach too long. My *new* family wanted to get packed up and on the road, headed back to their home, before it got to be too late in the day.

Alan and I were planning on stopping by to see our friend and favorite bartender, Charlene, at the restaurant we had visited Saturday night. I wanted to tell her about my *new* family. I had told her, through Facebook, we would be there that week and I had news to tell her, but I wanted to tell her my story, in person. I had become friends with this woman years before when we first purchased our timeshare and had visited her on each trip to Fort Lauderdale.

We asked Gayle and Dean and the children to stop by the restaurant again on their way back to the resort from the beach, so Charlene could meet them.

When they all arrived, I introduced my oldest daughter, Gayle, and Dean and my three grandchildren to Charlene, and she told us all our story was amazing. She didn't have all the details yet, but I told her I would give her more details as the week went on.

Gayle, Dean, and the children went to their room(s) to change and pack, and Alan and I talked a little while longer with Charlene.

"Your daughter is beautiful and your grandchildren are adorable!" Charlene said. She also said that she couldn't be happier for us, and she couldn't wait to hear the rest of our story and for us all to visit her again soon. She gave us her schedule for the week, and we told her we would probably be back later that day, after our family left to drive home.

Alan and I went back to our rooms to help our family load up their belongings.

Before they left, I told them I hoped perhaps the next time we got together, they could come to Arizona to visit—now that half of Gayle's *new* family lived in Arizona.

When they all drove away that afternoon, I was sad to see them go; but my heart was filled with great memories of our long holiday weekend together, and it was one of the best birthday presents I had ever received.

Chapter 27

More adventures and answered prayers

Now that our family had headed home, Alan and I had a few days to ourselves in Fort Lauderdale; and our friend, Rich, had also planned to come and stay with us for a couple of days before we flew back home. By Tuesday, weather reports were coming in that the hurricane in the Atlantic was not diminishing; and as it neared the continental states, there was a chance of the airports closing down as early as Friday evening. We knew we had to cut our vacation short again; so Tuesday morning, I changed our flight home to Arizona from Friday night to Friday morning— having reserved the last two seats available on the airplane. Our new flight would precipitate a stop in Austin, Texas on the way home, but we didn't care—we loved the Austin airport—and we were just thankful to have been able to change our flights.

The storm had already caused mass destruction in the Caribbean Islands, and friends of ours up and down the eastern and western coasts of Florida were preparing for severe storms and a possibility of electrical outages. Rich texted me, and said he would not make it down to Fort Lauderdale until Wednesday, because he was securing his house and his stepfather's house, before the weekend; but he still hoped to be able to stay for a couple of nights with us before we left.

With our plans for an early departure secure, we stopped by to talk to Charlene again; we spent the afternoon shopping and stopped at another one of our favorite *happy hour* spots to eat and relax.

We couldn't help but overhear the locals discussing the impending storm; the beach would be closing up for the weekend, and the restaurants were going to be shutting down on Friday night.

That evening, we planned to meet up with George and his girlfriend, Robbie, to listen to live music. We arrived at the club at eight, and George and Robbie arrived a short time later. We all sat and talked, waiting for the band to start at nine. At ten we asked the bartender what time the band was going to begin, and he replied, "Soon—maybe eleven? " It didn't sound like they were sure if there was a band showing up or not; and by midnight, there was still no live music yet, so we all left. Alan and I walked to a nice place nearby for a nightcap, where we waited for our ride back to our resort. Even without the live band, we'd had a great time hanging out with our *new friends*.

The next day, Wednesday, we spent the day watching retail shops and restaurants preparing for the storm; the sky was looking ominous and the ocean was churning, with seaweed scattered all across the beaches. The storm had ripped apart the Virgin Islands, and the Keys were preparing for the worst; even Miami was on high alert.

Back at the resort, we couldn't help notice all the vacationers swimming and hanging out around the pool and at the bar, as if they didn't have a care in the world. None of them seemed concerned at all about the impending storm.

I was still waiting to hear from Rich, regarding his arrival, but discovered he hadn't yet left his home in central Florida.

We asked the bartender at the pool bar if he had heard anything about the hotel closing for the weekend yet, and he said he had not; but he planned to drive his wife to Orlando after his work shift ended that day, so she and their one year old daughter could catch a flight to go stay with her parents in Baltimore. He told us every single flight out of Fort Lauderdale was booked already; I was so thankful that we had already moved our flights up earlier in the day Friday. The bartender thought the hotel would start telling guests they had to be out by Saturday morning, but when we returned to our room late that Wednesday afternoon, our telephone message light was blinking.

We listened to a recording, advising us that the Governor had ordered all non residents to evacuate the beach area by noon on Thursday. We were told we needed to check out by 10 am the following morning.

I contacted Rich with the news of our pending evacuation.

I wasn't sure what we were going to do until our flight left Friday morning, but since I had already contacted some old friends who still lived in the area, I texted my friend, Terrie. She had previously texted me and told me that we were welcomed to stay with her and her husband, Tom, if we were evacuated early. I asked if her offer was serious, and she reiterated it was. She and Tom offered to pick us up the next morning; she said we could stay with them for the night.

Thank you, God.

We went ahead and finished the laundry we had started and packed up all of our stuff. We showered and dressed and decided to return to the restaurant we had walked to the previous night, knowing they were still open and had an awesome *happy hour* and great food. On our way out of the hotel, we pre-checked out for the next morning, so we could just get up and leave.

On Thursday, Terri and Tom picked us up at the hotel and drove us back to their house. Terri worked from home that day and gave us her car to use, (which Tom had already filled with gas); and so we drove around, visiting my old neighborhoods. We found my old apartment—the one I had lived in with my mom in high school—it had been repainted; and I was surprised it was still standing (since the building was old when we lived in it—almost 40 years earlier)!

The neighborhood where we had lived with my aunt and uncle and cousins was still nice—Ruth's house no longer existed, but a new house had been built in its place. The private school she had attended was still at the end of the street, as was the 7-11; where we used to hang out, talking to the cute guys who worked there at night.

After we stopped for lunch, before we returned to Terri and Tom's house, we drove past a Tesla charging station— which was full of electric cars, trying to get a full charge before the storm. Every gas station we passed had a line out into the street with people trying to fill up all their cars with gas before the storm hit also.

We offered to take Terri and Tom out to eat dinner that evening, as a thank-you for their hospitality, wherever they wanted to go—before the restaurants started closing down for the weekend. We ended up at a casual little restaurant on the water, and saw that many of the yachts had been triple tied to the Intercostal Waterway docks. I wondered if that would even be enough to hold the boats in the water if there was a hurricane surge.

On the way back to their house, we drove by Terri and Tom's church; Tom had spent the afternoon helping to secure it in preparation for the storm. Back at their home, Terrie and I reminisced about our high school days, and then Alan and I finished re-packing.

We set the alarm for 6 am—everyone had been advised to arrive at the airport four hours before their scheduled flights.

Terrie and Tom drove us to the airport on Friday morning, and we thanked them for their generosity as we said our goodbyes.

Once inside the airport, we stepped into the long lines of people; hundreds, if not thousands of us, trying to evacuate before the hurricane hit. I had never seen so many people with small pets or people in wheelchairs at the airport before. Every gate was full, every flight was full, and every flight was delayed. We checked in our luggage and headed straight to the bar for breakfast, waiting for our flight and talking to all of the other people who were waiting with us. Even some of the bartenders told us they were trying to get out of Florida before the airport closed—which they were advised would be by 7 pm that evening.

I was so thankful we had been able to change our flights.

We'd chosen to eat breakfast at the bar in the restaurant right next to our gate, charging our cell phones and laptop until it was time to board. When we moved to our gate in advance of our scheduled departure, we discovered our gate number had been changed. We hurried to the next gate, and just as we found a place to sit, we found our gate had been changed again.

By the time we were in our seats on the plane, waiting in line on the runway to take off, I could not wait to leave Florida—something I don't think I had ever felt before.

We finally made it home late Friday afternoon, and went straight to our favorite Arizona restaurant for tacos. Technically, we were still on vacation, and there wasn't any food in the house. Once home from dinner, Alan practiced his music for his gig the next day—something he couldn't do while on vacation in Florida—and I watched the news reports, praying for all of my family and friends in Florida to be safe.

The next morning, Alan left early to hit the road for his gig, and I finished unpacking and doing laundry; I then headed out to the store. I made my usual stop at Starbucks for *breakfast* and spent the afternoon finishing laundry and working on my computer, mostly paying bills.

I pretended I was still on vacation, though alone, and took myself out to my favorite pizza restaurant for dinner and listened to a musical duo perform. I was doing anything I could to keep my mind off of the pending storm that was going to be hitting Florida and affecting all my family and friends there. Alan got home after midnight; and we stayed up, glued to the television once again, watching the weather reports to see what was happening with the hurricane.

I barely slept all night and got up early Sunday to get more updates.

There was a massive storm across the state, affecting both coasts, and everyone in my family and my family of friends got hit to some extent. Some friends had stayed with other friends who still had electricity, and my *new family* stayed with Dean's parents, along with his siblings and all their children.

Other than electrical outages, none of my family or friends had more than minimal damage to their homes and yards.

I did a lot of praying that weekend, asking God to keep my friends and family safe.

Once again, my prayers were answered.

Chapter 28

A union, a birthday, and destiny

September came to an end, we were back to our daily routines and anticipating the following month. My first daughter would be celebrating her birthday on the twenty-seventh, and I would actually be able to tell her, "Happy Birthday," for the first time in our lifetimes.

But first, my youngest daughter was getting married. She had planned her entire wedding, mostly by herself—while working full time—with a little help from her fiancé, friends, and her *other mothers*. These were the mothers of her two best friends, who had been there for her whenever she needed them and had treated her like one of their own most of her life.

The wedding ceremony was held on the beach and was spectacular. It was the best wedding I had ever attended! It wasn't just because it was my youngest daughter's wedding —it was just so perfect and had such a special, personal touch in every aspect. Rachel and Eddie had written their own personal vows and as Eddie first read his, we were all in tears. Rachel, somehow, was able to hold back the tears and read her vows, they exchanged rings, and surprised us all with a romantic dip kiss. Their reception started nearby, as they had pictures taken near the shore, with the sun setting over the ocean.

Then their music started, and the entire wedding party danced their way into the outdoor pavilion.

I had seen these two start dating as fourteen and fifteen year olds; they survived an adolescent crush, a friendship, and then years of separation. As adults, they got to know each other again through letters and phone calls, in a long distance relationship, and fell in love.

Everyone that was part of their lives and knew them, also knew they were perfect for each other. Their vows were that much more perfect because they were so truthful about their feelings.

Rachel and Eddie had chosen the resort for their reception and included their buffet; but they had personally chosen their own DJ and music, their own cake and flowers; and they had personally made all of their own decorations to give the venue a personal touch.

The wedding party and family spent the remainder of the weekend with the couple, celebrating their union because they had chosen to delay their honeymoon until the following summer.

Rachel had enrolled in the Masters program at her Nursing College and began classes the week after the wedding—to earn her MSN and become a Nurse Practitioner.

Rachel had invited her new sister, Gayle, to the ceremony; but Gayle explained to us all that she did not feel Rachel's and Eddie's wedding would be a good time for them to meet one another and our family and friends for the first time, as it would take away from all the attention that should only be on the bride that weekend. Gayle and Dean sent Rachel and Eddie a very thoughtful card and gift and wished them the best. Their thoughtfulness was the best gift they could have given the new couple.

After we returned from their destination wedding, I started texting Gayle and asked her where she would be on her birthday and what time she would be free to talk. I wanted to personally tell her, "Happy Birthday," this year. I messaged her on Facebook that morning, but that wasn't all I wanted to do—though it had been more than I had ever been able to do in the past. She contacted me and told me she would be free that afternoon, after lunch. We were able to talk for about fifteen or twenty minutes while I was on my lunch break. It was such an amazing experience— singing, *Happy Birthday,* over the phone to Gayle and not just to myself for the first time.

I had mailed her a card and some miscellaneous trinkets from Rachel's and Eddie's wedding, but nothing meant as much as actually finally knowing who my daughter was and being able to talk to her on her birthday.

I realized that afternoon that this was the first time—in 39 years—I had been able to actually say, "Happy Birthday," to my oldest daughter. The daughter who, as a baby, existed inside of me for four months, unknown to anyone and uninjured in a near fatal accident; the baby, who I talked to for months while I carried her; the baby I gave birth to but never saw before I gave her to another couple to raise. This was the little girl raised by an amazing family who treated her like a princess; the woman who grew up to be an intelligent and successful professional with an awesome family of her own.

That same year became the first year I was able to send Christmas presents to my three grandchildren, along with gifts for my oldest daughter and son-in-law in Florida—and I was also able to exchange gifts with Rachel and my new son-in-law, Eddie, in Arizona.

At that point, all I could do was thank God for answering my prayers.

I feel my life is now complete—I am a happy, content, and thankful mother of two awesome daughters and three adorable grandchildren. I also have two of the most amazing son-in-laws a mother could ask for, and I'm looking forward to more grandchildren in the future.

I can't say I could be much happier with my life than I am now. It may not be perfect; but I have a great job, my health, and a loving husband.

I am truly blessed!

Life can be challenging, and we all experience difficult times. But I've seen for myself that God does, in fact, answer prayers. Sometimes He does it suddenly, with the fluttering movements of a baby in the womb of her pregnant teen mother. Sometimes His answers take years to come, like when He chooses the perfect time to introduce that same mother to the woman she'd given to another couple as a baby to raise so many years before.

I've learned that when life's struggles get me down and being in the outside world sometimes scares me, I have to remind myself that God didn't put me on this earth to hide away from the world. He obviously had other plans for us when he saved my life, and the life of my baby, in a head on collision with a tree along the Natchez Trace Parkway.

I may feel partly cloudy at times, but each day that comes shows me just how bright and clear—and *Sunnie*—my life can be.

A special thanks to photographer, Marc Muench, for his amazing image of the Natchez Trace Parkway I was able to use for my book cover.

Check out his fine art photography @ marcmuench.com

Made in the USA
Middletown, DE
28 October 2021